AWAKE *to* Righteousness

Volume 1

A Study on the Book of Romans
Chapters 1 through 8

CONNIE WITTER

because of Jesus publishing

Awake to Righteous, Volume 1, Chapters 1 through 8

ISBN: 0-9883801-2-7

BECAUSE OF JESUS PUBLISHING
P.O. Box 3064
Broken Arrow, OK 74013

Cover design and layout: Nan Bishop, Tulsa, Oklahoma
nbishopsdesigns.com
Edited by Rose Karlebach, Tulsa, Oklahoma
onlyroseofsharon@gmail.com

Printed in the United States of America.

I dedicate this Bible study to my wonderful mom, Judy Beckham.

The very first person who told me the truth that I was "the righteousness of God in Christ Jesus" was you, Mom. Although I did not fully grasp its meaning at the time, a seed of truth was planted in my heart. This Bible Study is the fruit of you planting that truth in my heart and trusting Jesus to bring it out in my life.

Thank you so much for loving me and believing in me.

I love you and I am so blessed to call you Mom!

To those who faithfully attended the Because of Jesus Ministries Bible Study during the teaching of Awake to Righteousness. Your faithful attendance and support contributed to the writing of this book.

I especially want to thank:

Nancy Bishop, Art Director

Rose Karlebach, Editor

Thank you for using your gifts to contribute to the publishing of this Bible Study! You are both such a blessing to me!

Contents

Contents

A Personal Note from the Author

Welcome and thank you for joining me on this study of the Book of Romans, considered the most foundational book of the New Testament. For many years of my Christian life I read Romans with the veil of the law on my mind, and completely missed the liberating message of the true Gospel. Over time, as I asked the Holy Spirit to teach me and guide me into all truth, the scales were removed from my eyes and the glorious Good News about Jesus and His gift of righteousness became crystal clear! As I studied Romans in preparation for this verse-by-verse study, the Holy Spirit once again was faithful to reveal Jesus to me in a deeper way. The liberating truths that He revealed to me are the foundation of this wonderful study that I am about to share with you.

For far too long the church has been asleep in their righteousness, the god of this world blinding their eyes from the truth of their true identity in Christ. Sadly, the veil of the law keeps God's children bound up in guilt, shame, and condemnation. Romans 5:17 teaches us that as a result of Adam's sin, condemnation reigned in the hearts of all people, but the Good News is that those who receive the abundant provision of grace and the free gift of righteousness will triumph over sin and reign in life as kings through Jesus. When we awake to our righteousness in Christ, we live as the kings we were created to be.

In preparation for this study, I considered what it means to "awake to righteousness." The Disney movie, *The Lion King*, came to my mind as a perfect example. The main character of the story is a young lion cub, Simba, son of the mighty king, Mufasa. One day, acting in disobedience to his father, Simba finds himself caught in a life-threatening stampede. Seeing his son in grave danger, the great king runs out of the darkness to rescue his son from certain death, only to lose his own life in the process. As a result of his father's untimely death, the young cub is thrust into the premature position as king.

At the same time, Simba's jealous Uncle Scar has his own agenda, and makes a plan to steal the throne away from the young prince. He deceives Simba into believing that Simba is the one responsible for his father's death, and tells him that Mufasa would still be alive if Simba hadn't disobeyed. Feelings of guilt and condemnation make Simba run away and hide in shame, believing that he does not deserve his new position as king. For a season, Simba settles for a life in exile, lived as far less than who he truly is.

But the wise old baboon Rafiki, begins to speak to Simba about his true identity. "You don't even know who you are," the baboon says to the young prince, "but I have Good News for you. Your father is not dead, he's alive!" "Where?" Simba asks, unbelieving. "Come, I will show you!" Rafiki says as he motions to a nearby pond, revealing Simba's own reflection in the water. "See, there he is!" Rafiki says. "That's not my father; that's just my reflection," Simba denies. "No!" Rafiki interrupts, "Look harder. Your father is alive because he lives inside of you!"

As Simba looks down at his matured reflection in the water, he hears the echo of his father's voice, saying, "Simba, you have forgotten me." "No, Father! I would never forget you," Simba says, denying the truth of his father's statement. "Yes," Mufasa says to his beloved son, "you have forgotten who you are and so have forgotten me. . . . You are my son, and the one true king. . . . Remember who you are!" As Simba hears his father's words, he comes to realize that his act of disobedience could never steal his destiny from him, because it was never based on his behavior, but on his identity! As Simba awakens to who he truly is — the son of the king — all his condemnation, guilt and shame loses its control over him. Faith and courage rise up in Simba's heart as he chooses to embrace this gift from his father. No longer enslaved by the lies of his uncle, Simba wakes up to his true identity and begins to live as the king he had always been created to be!

What a powerful illustration of what it means to awake to righteousness and reign as a king in life through Jesus. Like Simba, you have a destiny awaiting you, as a beloved child of the King of kings! My prayer as we study Romans together, is that you too will awake to your righteousness, and experience the life-transforming power of God's grace. Don't settle for a mediocre life; live as the king you are destined to be!

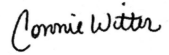

Connie Witter

1. To make the most of your group study experience, we suggest you purchase the *Awake to Righteousness* DVDs and downloadable *Leader's Guide* from the Because of Jesus website at www.becauseofJesus.com. A complete Bible Study Package is also available on our website for groups of ten (10) or more participants.
2. If you do have more than ten (10) participants in your group study, we suggest you have several discussion leaders, one for each group, with a maximum of ten (10) people per discussion group. Keep in mind that the smaller the discussion group, the more comfortable each person will be in participating, and in sharing from their heart. You can print off multiple copies of the *Leader's Guide* so that each group discussion leader has a copy.
3. Hand out the workbooks a week before the study begins so that each participant has an opportunity to get his or her lessons done before the first week's meeting. In this way, the DVDs will be a review of the lesson they have already done.
4. Pray before you put in the DVD. Ask the Lord to open your eyes to the truth, and acknowledge Him as your true teacher.
5. Each DVD lesson will take approximately 50 minutes to view. Encourage the participants to take notes while they are listening so they can share what the Lord has shown them during group discussion. You will learn so much from listening to one another and from hearing yourself say what the Lord has taught you. What you share not only encourages others, but helps solidify the truth in your own heart.
6. Once the DVD is finished, have the participants break up into discussion groups of ten (10) or less participants.
7. Begin group discussion by asking each person what the Holy Spirit specifically spoke to him or her through the DVD teaching that week.
8. Choose a few questions from each day's study to discuss in your group.
9. Ask for any prayer requests and end your study with a word of prayer.
10. At the end of each group discussion, encourage participants to spend time with the Lord and in His word over the next week, and remind them of which lesson they'll be studying the following week.

Week 1

The Good News is About Jesus

Romans 1:1-17

Day 1

The Good News is About Jesus

Day 2

Grace and Faith

Day 3

Salvation and Righteousness

Day 1

The Good News is About Jesus

Romans 1:1-17

1 This letter is from Paul, a slave of Christ Jesus, chosen by God to be an apostle and sent out to preach his Good News. 2 God promised this Good News long ago through His prophets in the holy Scriptures. 3 The Good News is about His Son. In His earthly life He was born into King David's family line.

ROMANS 1:1-3

Take time to pray before you begin.

Let's begin our exciting journey through Romans by asking the most important question concerning the Gospel: Who is this Gospel of Good News about?

In Romans 1:3 the Apostle Paul reveals this central truth: The Good News message is *always* about Jesus.

> Galatians 1:6-7: *6 I am shocked that you are turning away so soon from God, who called you to himself through the loving mercy of Christ. You are following a different way that pretends to be the Good News 7 but is not the Good News at all. You are being fooled by those who deliberately twist the truth concerning Christ.*

Paul is warning the Galatians about a "different" message being taught to them during his day, and we hear this same message being taught in churches today. It is a message that is all about *self*: self-improvement, self-effort, and self-righteousness. Its focus is not on Jesus, but rather on what "self" needs to do to earn God's blessing and favor. Although it pretends to be the Gospel, it's not the Gospel at all. The true Gospel is always about Jesus. If the message you are hearing is not about (a) who Jesus is, (b) what He has done for you on the cross, and (c) who you are in Him, it's not the Good News at all. The true Good News is always and only about Jesus.

The Pretend Gospel

This "pretend" gospel Paul is speaking about always focuses on man's performance. Its message to you is that you have to pray more, have more faith, quote more Scriptures, give more, be faithful to church and serve others more if you want to please God and receive

His blessing. Its focus is on what you lack, rather than on the completeness you have in Christ. While this other message tells you what you need to do in order to be righteous and holy, the true Good News Gospel tells you everything that Jesus did to make you righteous and holy. As you learn to recognize that the true Good News is all about Jesus, you'll be able to spot this counterfeit gospel very easily. Each time you hear a message preached ask yourself this question: "Is this message about Jesus? Is it about what He did for me and who I am in Him, or is it about what I need to do or what I am doing wrong?" If the focus is on you, then it's not the Good News. As we saw earlier in Romans 1:3, the true Good News is always about Jesus!

With that in mind, how can you distinguish the true Good News from the counterfeit?

Let's continue with Paul's thought, looking at another chapter in Galatians:

> Galatians 3:8-9: *8 What's more, the Scriptures looked forward to this time when God would declare the Gentiles to be righteous because of their faith. God proclaimed this good news to Abraham long ago when he said, "All nations will be blessed through you." 9 So all who put their faith in Christ share the same blessing Abraham received because of his faith.*

What was the Good News that God proclaimed to Abraham?

The True Good News

The true Good News that God proclaimed and promised to Abraham was about being made righteous through faith in Jesus. This Good News is revealed in every book of the Bible, from Genesis to Revelation, its earliest mention being in the Garden of Eden. When Adam and Eve failed, the Father spoke this promise to them, "I will send a Redeemer to redeem you," (Genesis 3:15). God talked to them about a seed (Jesus) who would come through a woman to redeem them and all of mankind. From the very beginning of the Bible, the Good News proclaimed that anyone who put their faith in the coming Redeemer would be declared righteous — not by their good works or performance — but through their faith in Jesus. Like the Apostle Paul warned, if you don't see Jesus in the Scriptures, you are not seeing the Truth. When you do see Jesus, you are seeing the Truth, and the Truth will always set you free!

In Luke 24:44 Jesus said, *"I told you that everything written about me in the law of Moses and the prophets and in the Psalms must be fulfilled."*

In John 5:39 Jesus said, *"You search the Scriptures because you think they give you eternal life. But the Scriptures point to Me!"*

What is the most important truth about the Gospel that Jesus shared in these two scriptures?

In these two verses, Jesus shared that the Scriptures are all about Him. Every passage of Scripture points to Jesus. When we read Scriptures and take the focus off of Jesus and what He's done for us, and instead focus on ourselves and what we need to do for Him, we become confused. When all you can see is what you have or have not done, you are not seeing the true Gospel, and it will bring condemnation to your heart. 2 Corinthians 3:6 says that the law kills and condemns, but the Spirit gives life.

I used to view the Scriptures as a list of dos and don'ts that I needed to live up to. By thinking this way brought condemnation to my heart because the focus wasn't on what Jesus had done for me, but rather on what I needed to do for Him. No matter how hard I tried, it seemed like I could never do enough.

> My journey to freedom began when I turned to Jesus with a simple prayer, "Lord, show me the Truth that will set me free." The Holy Spirit was faithful to me as He removed the veil of the law from my eyes and I began to see that the Good News is always about Jesus: what He has done for me and my new identity in Him.

My journey to freedom began when I finally turned to Jesus with a simple prayer, "Lord, show me the Truth that will set me free." The Holy Spirit faithfully removed the veil of the law from my eyes and I began to see that the Good News is always about Jesus: what He had done for me and my new identity in Him. I now ask the Holy Spirit to reveal Jesus to me each time I look at the Scripture. I know that when I see Jesus, I am seeing the Truth and it always brings freedom and liberty to my heart and life. As you study the scriptures, be encouraged that the very same passages which used to condemn your heart will now bring you life as you focus on Jesus!

Let's look at an example of what happens when we change the focus of our scripture reading from the law, to Jesus. Deuteronomy 28:1-66 is a passage that is familiar to most of us, all about the blessings and curses under the law. If you read it without understanding that the Good News is about Jesus, you'll think that your blessing is totally dependent on you and your ability to obey the law. "If you obey, you'll be blessed; but if you disobey, you'll be cursed". Since you know that you can't keep the law perfectly, your heart will condemn you and you'll believe that you have to suffer the curse! But if you read it knowing what Jesus has done for you under the New Covenant, you'll see that Jesus has redeemed you from the curse of the law, and qualified you for every one of His blessings, by making you righteous in Him! (Galatians 3:13-14) Relief will flood your soul as you realize that it's not your obedience that makes you righteous, but His (Romans 5:19). Remember, the Good News always points you to Jesus. It tells you (a) who Jesus is, (b) what He has done for you, and (c) who you are in Him! Knowing that Jesus has made you righteous as a free gift of His grace always brings joy and peace to your heart!

The true Gospel of Jesus Christ puts us all on the same level and in the same high place of honor as we place our faith in Him. It points us to Jesus and who we are in Him: righteous, wonderful, beloved children of God! We are all favored, qualified, innocent, and blameless in our Heavenly Father's eyes because of what Jesus has done for us. We are all very, very good in Christ, perfect and righteous in God's sight. Our righteousness is not based on anything we've done for Him, but based on everything Jesus has done for us. As we realize who we are in Jesus, we are empowered to love one another just like Jesus loves us. This is the power of the true Gospel: It is all about Jesus!

Now let's read Romans 1:4-7:

> Romans 1:4-5 *4 [And] he was shown to be the Son of God when he was raised from the dead by the power of the Holy Spirit. He is Jesus Christ our Lord. NLT 5 It is through Him that we have received grace (God's unmerited favor) and [our] apostleship to promote obedience to the faith and make disciples for His name's sake among all the nations. AMP*

> Romans 1:6-7 *6 And you are included among those Gentiles who have been called to belong to Jesus Christ. 7 I am writing to all of you in Rome who are loved by God and are called to be His own holy people. May God our Father and the Lord Jesus Christ give you grace and peace. NLT*

The first seven verses of Romans chapter 1 told us that the true Gospel is all about Jesus. In verses 8-15 Paul goes on to explain his desire to come in person to the people of Rome to share this Good News about Jesus with them, so that they can encourage each other in the faith.

> Romans 1:8-15: *8 Let me say first that I thank my God through Jesus Christ for all of you, because your faith in Him is being talked about all over the world. 9 God knows how often I pray for you. Day and night I bring you and your needs in prayer to God, whom I serve with all my heart by spreading the Good News about His Son. 10 One of the things I always pray for is the opportunity, God willing, to come at last to see you. 11 For I long to visit you so I can bring you some spiritual gift that will help you grow strong in the Lord. 12 When we get together, I want to encourage you in your faith, but I also want to be encouraged by yours. 13 I want you to know, dear brothers and sisters, that I planned many times to visit you, but I was prevented until now. I want to work among you and see spiritual fruit, just as I have seen among other Gentiles. 14 For I have a great sense of obligation to people in both the civilized world and the rest of the world, to the educated and uneducated alike. 15 So I am eager to come to you in Rome, too, to preach the Good News.*

In Romans 1:16-17: Paul again emphasizes that the Good News is about Jesus.

> Romans 1:16-17: *17 For I am not ashamed of the Gospel (good news) of Christ, for it is God's power working unto salvation, to everyone who believes with a personal trust and a confident surrender and firm reliance, to the Jew first and also to the*

Greek. 17 For in the Gospel a righteousness which God ascribes is revealed, both springing from faith and leading to faith... As it is written, The man who through faith is just and upright shall live by faith. AMP

Romans 1:17: *This Good News tells us how God makes us right in His sight. This is accomplished from start to finish by faith. As the Scriptures say, "It is through faith that a righteous person has life." NLT*

What does the Good News tell us? How is this accomplished?

___

___

The true Good News is about how God makes us righteous in His sight through our faith in what Jesus has done for us, not through our good works or performance.

* * *

Over the next two days, we will define four foundational words repeated by Paul in Romans 1:1-17, which will help us in our study of the Good News of Jesus Christ. They are: GRACE, FAITH, SALVATION, and RIGHTEOUSNESS. Our study of these words will free us from any misconceptions we may have regarding what Jesus really accomplished for us on the cross. As we learn to continually turn our focus from ourselves to Jesus, we will find ourselves awakening to righteousness and experiencing the abundant life He came to give us. Just like the Apostle Paul, our hearts will become convinced that the true Good News really is all and only about Jesus!

Grace and Faith

Romans 1:5, 16-17

It is through Jesus that we have received grace.
ROMANS 1:5

Take time to pray before you begin.

Romans 1:5 tells us that we have received grace through Jesus. But what exactly is grace? How would you describe *grace* to someone in your own words?

___

___

___

The New Covenant is described as the "Covenant of Grace". Sadly, for most believers grace is just a "Christianese" word that they really don't understand. Grasping its full meaning is essential to understanding the true Gospel and what Jesus accomplished for us on the cross.

The word *grace* (G5485) comes from the Greek word *charis.* According to Strong's, it is translated in the following ways: "acceptable, benefit, favour, gift, gracious, joy, liberality, pleasure, thanks," and "especially the divine influence upon the heart and its reflection in the life."

Grace is a Gift

When you accepted Jesus as your Savior, the Holy Spirit gave you a brand new heart (Ezekiel 36:26-27) This was a gift of God's love. You didn't earn it by your good works; you simply received it by faith in Jesus. You and I were once sinners, dead in our sin; but the Holy Spirit of grace made us alive in Christ, giving us a brand new identity by making us righteous in Jesus.

> Colossians 1:22 says: *Yet now He has reconciled you to himself through the death of Christ in his physical body. As a result, he has brought you into his own presence, and you are holy and blameless as you stand before Him without a single fault.*

Describe the new nature you were given by His grace.

___

___

Isn't it incredible that even though we have all sinned and still at times fail, Jesus has made you and me righteous, which means we are "blameless, holy and without fault" in our Heavenly Father's eyes? He has given us His very nature — a brand new identity — as a gift of grace. The transforming power of His grace is truly amazing. And it doesn't stop there!

Grace: The Transforming Power of the Holy Spirit Upon Your Heart

Grace is also the ongoing power of the Holy Spirit upon your mind, upon your thoughts, and upon your will, which brings what happened on the inside of you out for everyone to see. Grace is the power of the Holy Spirit producing the fruit of righteousness in your life.

2 Corinthians 1:12 defines grace as:

> *The grace of God (the unmerited favor and merciful kindness by which God, exerting his holy influence upon souls, turns them to Christ, and keeps, strengthens and increases them in Christian virtues). AMP*

In James 4:6 the Amplified Bible describes grace this way: *But He gives us more and more grace (power of the Holy Spirit, to meet this evil tendency and all others fully).*

According to these two verses, what is *grace* and how does it affect your life?

____

____

Grace strengthens you when you feel weak (2 Corinthians 12:9). It empowers you to overcome temptation (Hebrews 4:14-16). Grace influences your heart, turns you toward Jesus, and produces the fruit of the Spirit in your life (Galatians 5:22-23).

In 1 Corinthians 15:10, the Apostle Paul clearly describes the power of God's grace and what it produces in a person's life:

> *But by the grace (the unmerited favor and blessing) of God I am what I am, and His grace toward me was not [found to be] for nothing (fruitless and without effect). In fact, I worked harder than all of them [the apostles], though it was not really I, but the grace (the unmerited favor and blessing) of God which was with me. AMP*

Grace not only made you the righteous person you are in Jesus but it also empowers you to produce good fruit. As God's grace transforms your heart, it is also reflected in your life.

Have you ever been really discouraged about a circumstance in your life and called out to Jesus to help you? As new creations, we already have joy, peace, and love inside of us as part of our new nature in Jesus, but sometimes we don't feel like it. Grace is the "feel like it." It's the Holy Spirit influencing our emotions so that we feel like the person we truly are on the inside.

I can't count how many times I have felt negative emotions in my heart as I was tempted to be fearful, discouraged, or angry about a situation in my life. In each of these circumstances, as I've called upon Jesus, I have found my thoughts changing as a new perspective came to my heart which brought peace. There was no effort on my part to change myself, just a simple call to the One Who loves me and empowers me to think and act just like He does. This transformation was not in my own strength, but through His strength; not through my works, but through the work of His Holy Spirit in me.

Have you ever felt your heart change from discouragement to joy or from fear to peace after you prayed to Jesus for help? That's grace at work in your heart. Jesus *is* grace!

The Misconception About Grace

While *grace* is a word we hear often in Christian circles, many people have a very wrong idea about what it is and actually does. They believe the lie that, "If you teach too much grace it gives people a license to sin." They actually think teaching too much grace will promote sin! But the truth is revealed in 1 Corinthians 15:56 which says that *"the law gives sin its power." NLT* What they don't understand is that when people are taught the law — what they need to do or not do in order to be righteous and approved by God — it actually strengthens sin's power in their lives. On the other hand, when you teach people grace — who they already are because of what Jesus has done — it actually empowers them to live holy and godly lives.

> Titus 2:11-12: *11 For the grace of God (His unmerited favor and blessing) has come forward (appeared) for the deliverance from sin and the eternal salvation for all mankind. AMP 12 It teaches us to say, "No" to ungodliness and worldly passions, and to live self-controlled, upright and godly lives in this present age. NIV*

What has the *grace* of God come to do? (verse 11)

____

____

What does *grace* teach us and empower us to do? (verse 12)

____

____

The Truth About Grace

The truth is that Jesus brought us grace to deliver us from the power of sin, and to teach us to say, "No!" to sin because it is not who we are anymore. When we receive God's grace by relying on Jesus, we have the power of the Holy Spirit working in our hearts. The fruit of the Spirit is the Holy Spirit's power working in you to bring forth love, joy, peace, patience, goodness, kindness, gentleness, faith, and self-control. It is all a work of the Spirit!

When people don't know about the grace that is available to them through Jesus, the only thing left for them is self-reliance and self-effort. They live their entire lives trying to be good enough, yet feeling like failures, instead of relying upon Jesus and His strength within them. If we don't teach them grace, God's people will never live free! The true Good News is about relying upon Jesus.

Understanding the Spirit of Grace is what began my personal journey into freedom. For twenty years of my Christian life I had tried hard in my own strength to be good enough to earn God's blessing and approval. But each attempt only made me more aware of my failure. When I finally called out to Jesus to "show me the truth that would set me free," the Holy Spirit began to reveal Jesus to me. He showed me that I already was approved, righteous, and good in my Father's eyes because of Jesus. I came to realize that I didn't have to try to earn it anymore; my new nature was a gift of His grace.

As I continued in this new understanding of grace, the Holy Spirit taught me to rely upon Jesus and His strength within me every single day. I could quit relying on myself and my own human effort to be good. Whenever I was tempted, all I needed to do was look to Jesus, and the Spirit of grace would bring out the fruit in my life. As I learned to exchange my self-reliance for the power of the Holy Spirit working in me, my life began to be transformed. I realized I could do nothing in my own strength, but to receive His grace, all I had to do was continually rely upon Jesus!

Faith Means to Rely Upon Jesus

> Romans 1:17: *This Good News tells us how God makes us right in His sight. This is accomplished from start to finish by faith. As the Scriptures say, "It is through faith that a righteous person has life."*

Verse 17 in the Amplified Bible says: *As it is written, The man who through faith is righteous shall live by faith.*

Faith comes from the Greek word "*pistis*" (G4102 Strong's) and it means "reliance upon Christ for salvation; constancy in such profession."

Romans 1:5 says, *"It is through Him that we have received grace (God's unmerited favor) and [our] apostleship to promote obedience to the faith. AMP*

The words "obedience to the faith" in this verse mean "an attentive hearkening to relying upon Jesus for salvation" (G5218 Strong's). Obedience in the New Covenant actually means "to rely upon Jesus". Disobedience in the New Covenant is to rely upon yourself!

True Obedience in the New Covenant is Relying Upon Jesus

> 1 John 3:22-23: *22 And we will receive from him whatever we ask because we obey him and do the things that please him. NLT 23 And this is His order (His command...that we should believe in (put our faith and trust in and adhere to and rely on) the name of His Son Jesus Christ (the Messiah), and that we should love one another, just as He has commanded us. AMP*

Day 2

What is the command of the New Covenant?

____

____

How can you obey God and do what pleases Him?

____

____

The command of the New Covenant is really simple and clear. *Disobedience* in the New Covenant is relying upon yourself for your righteousness, provision, approval, favor, blessing, and strength. *Obedience* in the New Covenant is relying upon Jesus for your righteousness, provision, approval, blessing, favor, and strength to love others the way He loves us. It's relying upon Jesus every moment of every day. You never stop relying on Jesus and what He's done for you. That, my friend, is what it means to live by faith!

In addition, faith also means "constancy in such profession." It means you are in constant agreement with the Father's view of you in Christ. When you live by faith, you are constantly relying upon Jesus for everything you need, and speaking in agreement with who you are in Him. For instance, "I'm blessed because of Jesus;" "I'm righteous because of Jesus;" "I'm innocent and blameless and healed and whole and complete because of Jesus." That's faith because you are relying upon Jesus and not yourself.

So let's read Romans 1:16 with this in mind:

> *For I am not ashamed of the Gospel of Jesus Christ, for it is God's power (His grace) working unto salvation . . . to everyone who believes with a personal trust and a confident surrender of their own ability to save themselves and firmly relies upon Jesus." [Author's Paraphrase]*

That "confident surrender" is a confident surrender of your self-reliance. Have you ever heard somebody say, "It's not working for me"? If it's not working, if you're not experiencing peace, joy, confidence and security, it's because instead of continuing to rely upon Jesus and His gift of righteousness, you begin to rely upon yourself.

The Misconception of Faith

You may have been wrongly taught that it was your responsibility to have enough faith and that it depended upon your ability to believe. Thinking this way places all the focus on you and takes all the focus off of Jesus. For me faith had become something I had to "do" to earn God's blessing. Words like, "I just don't have enough faith;" "I need more faith," "I'll never have as much faith as she has," constantly kept the focus on me. I would often think, "If I just had enough faith, then I'd qualify for God's blessings." I had completely lost sight of Jesus, thinking it was all about me and what I had to do. But true faith is "relying upon Jesus," and a constant profession of who He is, and who He says we are, in Him.

Day 2

The Truth About Faith

Hebrews 12:2: *Looking unto Jesus, the author and finisher of our faith. NKJV*

True faith is a simple child-like call upon Jesus for salvation in every situation and circumstance of our lives. It is acknowledging what Jesus has done for us, and who we are in Him. Many of us have thought that it's up to us to muster up this faith, but the truth is that He is the Author and Finisher of our faith. Our part is just to fix our eyes on Him realizing that we can't do it on our own, and that He is our Savior.

The Good News tells us that being made right in God's sight starts by faith (relying upon Jesus), and it finishes by faith (relying upon Jesus). "For the righteous shall live by faith (relying upon Jesus)." Whenever you see the word "faith" in the Bible, remember that it means "reliance upon Jesus for salvation." As you do this, you will find your focus turning away from your ability to believe, to His ability in you, and you'll experience His grace empowering you to trust Him with all of your heart!

Humbly come to Him and receive His grace to believe, "Lord, I confidently surrender my ability to have enough faith. I can't do it in my own strength and self-effort. I am helpless without You, Lord. I need Your grace to trust You."

> Matthew 6:6: *"Here's what I want you to do: Find a quiet, secluded place so you won't be tempted to role-play before God. Just be there as simply and honestly as you can manage. The focus will shift from you to God, and you will begin to sense his grace. MSG*

Salvation and Righteousness

Romans 1:16-17

Take time to pray before you begin.

Today as we finish up Week 1 of our study of Romans, we'll be looking at two of the most foundational words in the Bible. Without understanding these words we can never truly comprehend why the Gospel is such Good News. These words are *salvation* and *righteous*ness.

Salvation

The word *salvation* comes from the Greek work *soteria* (G4991 Strong's; Thayer's) and it denotes "deliverance; preservation; wholeness." It is "the present experience of God's power to deliver from the bondage of sin, inclusively, to sum up all the blessings bestowed by God on men in Christ through the Holy Spirit." (Vine's New Testament)

With this definition in mind, how would you explain salvation?

____

____

____

Let's read two scriptures for further clarity:

> Romans 1:16: *For I am not ashamed of the Gospel (good news) of Christ, for it is God's power working unto <u>salvation</u>...to everyone who believes with a personal trust and a confident surrender and firm reliance, to the Jew first and also to the Greek. AMP*
>
> Ephesians 2:8: *For it is by free grace (God's unmerited favor) that you are saved (delivered from judgment and made partakers of Christ's salvation) through [your] faith. And this <u>[salvation]</u> is not of yourselves [of your own doing, it came not through your own striving], but it is the gift of God. AMP*

What is the power of the Gospel? And how does salvation come into a person's life? (Romans 1:16)

____

____

How does Ephesians 2:8 define the word "saved"?

The Misconception and Truth About Salvation

Many Christians have a very limited idea of what salvation actually is. They think it is merely deliverance from hell, and a ticket into heaven. While that is certainly true, salvation is so much more! It is our deliverance from the bondage and judgment of sin, and an invitation to partake of every blessing bestowed upon us in Christ while we live here on earth. When you were saved you were delivered from every curse of the law that you would have deserved as a result of your disobedience, and now you have been made a partaker of every promised blessing of God. This salvation is a gift of God that has come to you as a result of Jesus' obedience on your behalf.

From now on when you see the word *salvation* in the Bible, remember that it includes every blessing and promise that you have in Christ. Forgiveness, deliverance, peace, joy, healing, prosperity, favor, wisdom, and guidance are all part of your salvation package in Christ.

Righteousness

Romans 1:17: *This Good News tells us how God makes us right in His sight. This is accomplished from start to finish by faith. As the Scriptures say, "It is through faith that a righteous person has life."*

Romans 1:17: *For in the Gospel a righteousness which God ascribes is revealed, both springing from faith and leading to faith.... As it is written, The man who through faith is just and upright shall live and shall live by faith. AMP*

What does the Good News tell you?

Righteousness means: "innocent; free from guilt or blame; justified" (Strong's 1342, 1343, 1344)

So what does it mean that we are justified?

It is the judicial act of God, by which he pardons all the sins of those who believe in Christ, and accounts, accepts, and treats them as righteous in the eye of the law.... In addition to the pardon of sin, justification declares that all the claims of the law are satisfied.... The law is not relaxed or set aside, but is declared to be fulfilled in the strictest sense; and so the person justified is declared to be entitled to all the advantages and rewards arising from perfect obedience to the law (Romans 5:1-10). It proceeds on the ... crediting to the believer by God himself of the perfect righteousness ... of Jesus Christ (Romans 10:3-9). Justification is not the forgiveness of a man without righteousness, but a declaration that he possesses a righteousness which perfectly and forever satisfies the law, namely, Christ's righteousness (2 Corinthians 5:21; Romans 4:6-8). www.christiananswers.net/dictionary/justification.html:Bible Encyclopedia

According to this definition, what does it mean to be declared righteous in Jesus?

____

____

The Misconception About Righteousness

One of the biggest misunderstandings about righteousness is that the righteous are supposed to live and be blessed by their obedience to the law. They believe that even though Jesus made you righteous, you have to keep yourself righteous by your good works. But any effort on your part to earn God's blessing through your obedience is simply self-reliance. It's an attempt to make yourself righteous instead of relying upon Jesus for His righteousness, and resting in the truth that you are blessed because of Him. Any time a person depends on their own obedience to the law to make them approved and blessed by God, they are depending on their own self-righteousness. The power of the Gospel will never work in the life of a person who is relying upon himself. The power of the Gospel only works salvation (peace, joy, wisdom, healing, provision, etc.) in the lives of those who rely on the truth that they are righteous because of Jesus.

In spite of the fact that I had been saved by grace, for many years I believed the lie that I had to earn every other blessing and favor of God by my own good works. So I depended on my giving, my faithful church attendance, my faith, my tithing, and my attempts to obey God's word to qualify myself for His blessing. But doing this only led to me being disappointed and frustrated because it became apparent to me that the power of the Gospel was not working in my life. I was not experiencing the peace, joy and financial provision that God had promised.

> As I turned to Him for the truth, I began to understand that righteousness is a gift of God's grace.

Thank goodness, Jesus didn't leave me in that frustrating place. As I turned to Him for the truth, I began to understand that righteousness is a gift of God's grace. As I began relying upon Jesus instead of myself, the power of the Gospel began working in my life. After it finally dawned on me that I could never earn His blessing by my good works, I surrendered my self-reliance and embraced the truth that it is Jesus who qualifies me for every blessing of God.

Righteousness was given to me by faith (trusting and relying upon Jesus) and now I daily experience the benefits of salvation. You and I can rest in Jesus' obedience, knowing the Holy Spirit will do the work in us and bring forth the fruit of righteousness in our lives.

Day 3

The Truth about Righteousness

When you were made righteous through your faith in Jesus, your Heavenly Father declared you innocent and free from all guilt and blame in His sight forever! He pardoned all your sins and justified you in the eye of the law. He did this by giving you the perfect righteousness of Jesus Christ, which qualifies you for all the rewards and advantages of perfectly obeying the law. But think about it, did you obey the law perfectly? No, of course not! That's why righteousness is a gift.

You have been declared righteous by God Himself. You don't have to try to earn His blessing or qualify yourself anymore. You've been given — as a gift — the perfect obedience of Jesus Christ, which has been imputed to your account. When the Father looks at you, He does not see a sinner. He sees His beloved child who is qualified, holy, blameless and without fault in His sight because of your faith in Jesus! You are blessed not because of what you do, but because of what Jesus did for you! That's what it means to be declared righteous in Jesus!

So, let's read Romans 1:16-17 with our new understanding of these four wonderful words: GRACE, FAITH, SALVATION, and RIGHTEOUSNESS:

Romans 1:16-17: 16 *I am not ashamed of the Gospel ... of Jesus Christ for it is God's power (the transforming power of Grace) working unto salvation (deliverance from sin, forgiveness, peace, provision, healing, approval, wisdom, guidance, joy, love, self-control) to everyone who believes with a personal trust and confident surrender of his own ability to save himself and relies completely on Jesus. 17 This Good News tells us that God makes us righteous (innocent, free from all blame and guilt, and qualified for every blessing) in His sight by relying upon Jesus. This begins by relying upon Jesus and ends by relying upon Jesus. The righteous shall live by relying upon Jesus for everything they need. [Author's Paraphrase of AMP and NLT]*

This then, is the Good News about Jesus and is the foundation for our study of the Book of Romans.

So Awake to Righteousness!

Jesus, I surrender my self-reliance and self-effort and completely rely upon You as my righteousness! I can't earn Your approval and blessing by my good works. They are a gift of grace to me because You love me! I can't change myself, but the transforming power of Your grace is at work in me as I live by continually relying upon You, Jesus, for salvation in every area of my life!

What is the main truth you learned from today's study?

____

____

____

Self-Righteousness vs Jesus-Righteousness

Romans 1:18-3:31

Day 1

A Condemned Mind: Exchanging the Truth for a Lie

Day 2

Self-Righteousness

Day 3

Jesus-Righteousness

Day 1

A Condemned Mind: Exchanging the Truth for a Lie

Romans 1:18-32

Take time to pray before you begin.

Today we'll take a look at Romans 1:18-31, but let's first recall what we learned in Week 1 concerning the Good News about Jesus.

> Romans 1:16: *For I am not ashamed of this Good News about Christ. It is the power of God (His grace) at work, saving everyone who believes – the Jew first and also the Gentile.*

> Romans 1:17: *This Good News tells us how God makes us right [forgiven and qualified] in His sight. This is accomplished from start to finish by faith [relying upon Jesus]. As the Scriptures say, "It is through faith [relying upon Jesus] that a righteous person has life. [Author's Inserts]*

After the Apostle Paul explains the Good News about Jesus, he begins to talk about what happens in a person's life when they reject this Good News and go about living life on their own. He shares how the Good News about Jesus is that we've been made righteous through faith and not through our own good works. When we reject this righteousness that God offers through Jesus it leads to a condemned mind which produces a sin depraved life. Without Jesus, all men are unrighteous and under the power of sin.

> Romans 1:18: *But God shows His anger from heaven against all sinful, wicked people who suppress the truth by their wickedness.*

If you read this verse without a clear understanding of our New Covenant of Grace in Christ, you might get the wrong idea that God is still angry at sinners. While it is true that in the Old Covenant (which was based on the law), the wrath and anger of God was poured out upon sin, in the New Covenant (which is based on grace), the wrath and anger of God has been poured out once and for all upon Jesus (Isaiah 53:4-12). So now we are no longer under the wrath and indignation of God, but we are under His grace.

> Ephesians 2:1-5: *1 And you [He made alive], when you were dead (slain) by [your] trespasses and sins. 2 In which at one time you walked [habitually]. You were following the course and fashion of this world [were under the sway of the tendency of this present age], following the prince of the power of the air. [You were obedient to and under the control of] the [demon] spirit that still constantly works in the sons of disobedience... 3 Among these we as well as you once lived and conducted ourselves in*

the passions of our flesh [our behavior governed by our corrupt and sensual nature], obeying the impulses of the flesh and the thoughts of the mind [our cravings dictated by our senses and our dark imaginings]. We were then by nature children of [God's] wrath and heirs of [His] indignation, like the rest of mankind. 4 But God—so rich is He in His mercy! Because of and in order to satisfy the great and wonderful and intense love with which He loved us, 5 Even when we were dead (slain) by [our own] shortcomings and trespasses, He made us alive together in fellowship and in union with Christ; [He gave us the very life of Christ Himself, the same new life with which He quickened Him, for] it is by grace (His favor and mercy which you did not deserve) that you are saved (delivered from judgment and made partakers of Christ's salvation). AMP

Ephesians 2:8: *For it is by free grace (God's unmerited favor) that you are saved (delivered from judgment and made partakers of Christ's salvation) through [your] faith. And this [salvation] is not of yourselves [of your own doing, it came not through your own striving], but it is the gift of God. AMP*

What was true of all of us at one time? (verses 1-3)

____

____

Why did God save us from our sin, and how did He do it? (verses 4-5,8)

____

____

We were all, at one time, dead in our sins. Because of God's intense and wonderful and great love with which He loved us, even when we were sinners, Jesus died for us to make us righteous. Jesus took the punishment and condemnation that we deserved. He saved us from judgment and made us partakers of His salvation. That's the Good News about Jesus.

Isaiah 54:9-10: *9 "Just as I swore in the time of Noah that I would never again let a flood cover the earth, so now I swear that I will never again be angry and punish you. 10 For the mountains may move and the hills disappear, but even then My faithful love for you will remain. My covenant of blessing will never be broken," says the LORD.*

What promise did your Heavenly Father give you in this verse?

____

____

From now on when you read verses in the Bible that are talking about the wrath and anger of God, remember the Good News about Jesus. When people have asked me about verses in the Bible that refer to the anger and wrath of God, I say, "Do you not know what Jesus did for us? Jesus took the penalty for our sins. Sin has a payment. The wages of sin is death, but Jesus paid it so that we could be made righteous in God's sight. That's why He came."

So, don't ever again believe the lie that God is still angry because of man's sin; instead believe His promise in Christ. When you see the rainbow in the sky, it's not just a reminder that God will never again flood the earth, it's also His personal promise to you that He will never be angry at you again because of Jesus! You'll be confused if you read Scriptures on the wrath and anger of God and forget about Jesus, but if you will remember what Jesus did for you, you'll never be confused about the Good News again!

Rejecting the Truth Produces a Condemned Mind

Romans 1:19-32:

19 They know the truth about God because he has made it obvious to them. 20 For ever since the world was created, people have seen the earth and sky. Through everything God made, they can clearly see his invisible qualities – his eternal power and divine nature. So they have no excuse for not knowing God. 21 Yes, they knew God, but they wouldn't worship Him as God or even give him thanks. And they began to think up foolish ideas of what God was like. As a result, their minds became dark and confused.

22 Claiming to be wise, they instead became utter fools. 23 And instead of worshiping the glorious, ever-living God, they worshiped idols made to look like mere people and birds and animals and reptiles. NLT 24 So God let these people go their own way. They did what they wanted to do, and their filthy thoughts made them do shameful things with their bodies. CEV 25 <u>They traded the truth about God for a lie.</u> So they worshiped and served the things God created instead of the Creator Himself, who is worthy of eternal praise! Amen. NLT 26 God let them follow their own evil desires. Women no longer wanted to have sex in a natural way, and they did things with each other that were not natural. CEV 27 And the men also turned from natural relations with women and were set ablaze . . . with lust for one another — men committing shameful acts with men and suffering in their own bodies and personalities the inevitable consequences and penalty of their wrong-doing. . . . 28 And so, since they did not see fit to acknowledge God or approve of Him or consider Him worth the knowing, God gave them over to a base and <u>condemned mind</u> to do things not proper or decent but loathsome. AMP 29 Their lives became full of every kind of wickedness, sin, greed, hate, envy, murder, quarreling, deception, malicious behavior, and gossip. 30 They are backstabbers, haters of God, insolent, proud, and boastful. They invent new ways of sinning, and they disobey their parents. 31 They refuse to understand, break their promises, are heartless, and have no mercy. 32 They know God's justice requires that those who do these things deserve to die, yet they do them anyway. Worse yet, they encourage others to do them, too. NLT

When a person takes on their own opinion about God instead of believing the Truth, what happens to their mind? (verse 21)

____

____

____

What does verse 24 tells us about the free choice of man?

____

God gives everyone a free choice to either rely upon Jesus for their righteousness or to rely upon themselves. When men reject the Good News about Jesus it leads to a sin depraved life. When a person begins to think up foolish ideas about God and take on their own opinion instead of believing the truth, their mind becomes dark and confused.

What kind of mind does a person have who exchanges the truth for a lie? (verses 25-28)

____

____

What are some of the actions that come from a condemned mind? (verses 28-32)

____

____

Exchanging the Truth for a Lie

Romans 1:18-32 reveals the depravity that sin brings when a person exchanges the truth for a lie. The truth is that righteousness is available to every man through relying upon Jesus. But when men reject that truth for a lie and rely upon themselves, it produces a condemned mind. The Apostle Paul is showing here what condemnation and sin do to the people God loves, and that the only answer to this state of condemnation and sin is Jesus and His gift of righteousness.

Even as a believer, if you exchange the truth (that you are righteous, qualified, approved, and blessed because of Jesus) with the lie (that you are not good enough or qualified because of your failures), you will live with a condemned mind.

So what exactly is a condemned mind? A condemned mind is a negative mindset that embraces a lie about God and yourself. A condemned mind creates a state of hopelessness, which empowers sin, and sin creates depravity, heartache and pain. Jesus came to set us free and to deliver us from this cycle of condemnation, and the power of sin.

In order for you to understand what a condemned mind is, I want to share a personal example of exchanging the truth for a lie and how it affected my heart and life.

When I first started teaching Bible Study, I was a nervous wreck. Even though the truth was that Jesus had anointed and qualified me to preach the Good News, I believed the lie that I was inadequate and unqualified to teach anyone. As a result, it created insecurity,

Day 1

fear, and anxiety in my heart. Embracing my opinion over God's opinion of who I am in Christ resulted in me having a condemned mind. Even though my Heavenly Father didn't condemn me, I condemned myself because I chose to believe the lie. Keep in mind that when you exchange the truth for a lie, your mind is condemned, and it produces depression, discouragement, fear, and worry and keeps you in the vicious cycle of sin.

But all that changed when I decided that I wanted to be free, and I surrendered my opinion of myself and began to embrace God's opinion of me. His grace was there to deliver me from all my fears. I repented of my wrong way of thinking, turned my focus to Jesus and said, "Father, I give up the lie I have believed and I embrace the truth of what You say about me." As I began to agree with the truth — that I am anointed and qualified to preach the Good News because of Jesus — my heart was set free from insecurity. Now I boldly and confidently proclaim the Good News without fear because I know and have experienced the truth that Jesus came to set me free from a condemned mind. Just as believing the lie produces sin and depravity, believing the truth produces the fruit of righteousness and blessing in your life. Condemnation dissipates when you embrace the truth of who you are in Jesus, and the glory of God shines forth in every area of your life.

What causes a condemned mind?

____

____

How can you live free from condemnation and its effect on your life?

____

____

____

Self-Righteousness

Romans 2

Take time to pray before you begin.

In Romans 1:18-32, the Apostle Paul taught how a condemned mind is the result of exchanging the truth for a lie. We learned that a condemned mind leads to sin and depravity.

In Chapter 2, Paul addresses the self-righteous; those who look down on others. These are the people who are trying to be made righteous in God's sight through their obedience to the law. They rely upon themselves instead of Jesus.

> Romans 2:1: *You may think you can condemn such people, but you are just as bad, and you have no excuse! When you say they are wicked and should be punished, you are condemning yourself, for you who judge others do these very same things.*

According to Romans 2:1, when a person judges and condemns others, who are they also condemning?

____

As we read through this passage of Scripture, remember that the Apostle Paul is addressing self-righteous people who believe the lie that it is their good works that make them righteous before God. He's saying, "You may think you can condemn others for sinning and not living a perfect life, but you don't live a perfect life either! In fact, you do the very same sinful things they do." The list of sins he talks about in Romans 1:27-31 includes quarreling, strife, lying, jealousy and gossip.

Paul is making the point that a person who judges and condemns another person because of their bad behavior is also condemning himself, because we all have times when we behave badly. When we are self-righteous, we think that it's our good behavior that makes us righteous before God. When we condemn those around us whom we think are not behaving as well as we are, indirectly we are condemning ourselves. Those same negative thoughts you have toward someone who has failed, are the same negative thoughts you will have about yourself when you fail.

I have come to realize that when I begin to judge or condemn a person because of a particular behavior that I think is wrong, it is an indicator that I am actually depending on my good behavior to make me righteous before God. The problem with this kind of thinking is that inevitably I will fail, and when I do I will judge myself unworthy and unqualified as well. The only way to stay free from self-condemnation is to realize that it's only because of Jesus that you are qualified and blessed! When you truly embrace this truth, compassion — instead of judgment — will be the fruit of your life toward others who are struggling!

Romans 2:2-3: *And we know that God, in his justice, will punish anyone who does such things. 3 Since you judge others for doing these things, why do you think you can avoid God's judgment when you do the same things?*

Keep in mind, as you read these verses, the Apostle Paul was talking to people who were living under the law. The law says, "DO GOOD, GET GOOD; DO BAD, GET BAD. OBEY, BE BLESSED; DISOBEY, BE CURSED." The penalty of our sin is punishment under the law. He's explaining that under the law, all men get what their actions deserve. Without Jesus, man pays the penalty for his own sin. But keep in mind that we are no longer under the law. Because of Jesus, we are under God's grace. We no longer get what we deserve. We receive God's undeserved blessing and favor because of Jesus! Many people have read this chapter of the Bible and have become confused and condemned because they didn't understand who the Apostle Paul was talking to. He was addressing the self-righteous people so that they would understand that their own good works could never make them righteous before God. Their only hope was to rely upon Jesus and receive the gift of righteousness that He offers. If you will keep this in mind as you read Romans 2, you won't be confused.

Romans 2:4: *Don't you see how wonderfully kind, tolerant, and patient God is with you? Does this mean nothing to you? Can't you see that <u>His kindness</u> is intended to turn you from your sin?*

The New King James Versions says: *Or do you despise the riches of His goodness, forbearance, and longsuffering, not knowing that the goodness of God leads you to repentance? NKJV*

What turns us from our sin and leads us to repent?

____

In this verse Paul explained that telling people that God was angry with them and judging them badly would not turn them from their sin. Rather, sharing the Good News about God's love and kindness, which He demonstrated by offering them His gift of righteousness through Jesus, causes them to turn from their sins. That's what changes a person's mind from relying upon themselves, to relying upon Jesus.

Romans 3:23-24: *For everyone has sinned; we all fall short of God's glorious standard. 24 Yet, God with His undeserved kindness, declares that we are righteous. He did this through Christ Jesus when He freed us from the penalty of our sins.*

How did God show His kindness toward us?

____

It's the undeserved kindness of God; the Good News that He made us right in His sight through Jesus Christ and freed us from the penalty of our sin, that causes people to turn away from a sin-depraved, condemning life into the arms of a loving Heavenly Father. It's not the judgment of God, but the goodness of God that leads men to repentance.

In the following verses, the Apostle Paul continues to explain the terms of the law:

> Romans 2:5-24: *5 But because you are stubborn and refuse to turn from your sin, you are storing up terrible punishment for yourself. For a day of anger is coming, when God's righteous judgment will be revealed.*
>
> Verse 6: *He will judge everyone according to what they have done.*
>
> Verse 7: *He will give eternal life to those who keep on doing good, seeking after the glory and honor and immortality that God offers. 8 But He will pour out his anger and wrath on those who live for themselves, who refuse to obey the truth and instead live lives of wickedness. 9 There will be trouble and calamity for everyone who keeps on doing what is evil – for the Jew first and also for the Gentile. 10 But there will be glory and honor and peace from God for all who do good – for the Jew first and also for the Gentile. 11: For God does not show favoritism. 12 When the Gentiles sin, they will be destroyed, even though they never had God's written law. And the Jews, who do have God's law, will be judged by that law when they fail to obey it. 13 For merely listening to the law doesn't make us right with God. It is obeying the law that makes us right in His sight.*
>
> Verse 14: *Even Gentiles, who do not have God's written law, show that they know his law when they instinctively obey it, even without having heard it. 15 They demonstrate that God's law is written in their hearts, for their own conscience and thoughts either accuse them or tell them that they are doing right.*
>
> 16: *And this is the message I proclaim – that the day is coming when God, through Christ Jesus, will judge everyone's secret life. 17 You who call yourselves Jews are relying on God's law, and you boast about your special relationship with him. 18 You know what he wants; you know what is right because you have been taught his law. 19 You are convinced that you are a guide for the blind and a light for a people who are lost in darkness. 20 You think you can instruct the ignorant and teach children the ways of God. For you are certain that God's law gives you complete knowledge and truth. 21 Well then, if you teach others, why don't you teach yourself? You tell others not to steal, but do you steal? 22 You say it is wrong to commit adultery, but do you commit adultery? You condemn idolatry, but do you use items stolen from pagan temples? 23 You are so proud of knowing the law, but you dishonor God by breaking it. 24 No wonder the Scriptures say, "The Gentiles blaspheme the name of God because of you."*

Look at verse 17. Who is the Apostle Paul talking to? What are they relying upon?

____

This passage of Scripture reveals very clearly that the Apostle Paul was addressing the Jews who were relying upon the law to make themselves righteous. He was making a very clear point that no one obeys the law perfectly so no one can ever be made righteous by trying to obey it.

Under the law, how are people judged? (verses 6-10)

____

____

Look at verse 13. How does one become righteous based on the law?

____

____

In this verse, Paul explains that under the terms of the law, you had to obey the law perfectly to be righteous (Deuteronomy 6:24-25), but in Romans 3:20-22, He makes it clear that under grace, no one will ever be made righteous by obeying the law, but only through faith in Jesus.

Verses 7-10 explain that under the law those who do evil will be judged and those who do good will receive eternal life. However, Romans 3:12 says that without Jesus, ***no one does good, not a single one.*** With this in mind, how many of us qualify for eternal life by our own goodness?

____

If you stand before God based on the law, then you'll take the penalty for your own sin. The Good News is that Jesus took the penalty for your sin so you don't have to. All you have to do is rely on Jesus. Under the law, God judges people according to what they have done, but under grace, God judges people based on what Jesus has done. Under the law, everyone is judged a failure, but under grace, everyone who relies upon Jesus is judged righteous, innocent, and perfect in the Father's eyes! That is the Good News about Jesus!

In this next passage of Scripture the Apostle Paul clearly explains the impossibility of trying to be made righteous before God through our own obedience to the law. We all need a Savior. He makes it very clear why the gift of righteousness through faith in Jesus is really Good News!

> Romans 2:25-29: *25 The Jewish ceremony of circumcision has value only if you obey God's law. But if you don't obey God's law, you are no better off than an uncircumcised Gentile. 26 And if the Gentiles obey God's law, won't God declare them to be His own people? 27 In fact, uncircumcised Gentiles who keep God's law will condemn you Jews who are circumcised and possess God's law but don't obey it. 28 For you are not a true Jew just because you were born of Jewish parents or because you have gone through the ceremony of circumcision. 29 No, a true Jew is one whose heart is right with God. And true circumcision is not merely obeying the letter of the law; rather, it is a change of heart produced by God's Spirit. And a person with a changed heart seeks praise from God, not from people.*

Look at verse 29. What is the truth that the Apostle Paul is teaching in Romans Chapter 2?

___

___

In verse 29 the Apostle Paul clearly explained the whole point of what he is teaching in Romans chapter 2. He says, "You Jews are trying to be righteous and qualified through your obedience to the law. But it's not your obedience to the law that makes you righteous, it's a change of heart; a change of identity that is produced by the Spirit. The only way to be made righteous before God is by relying upon Jesus."

In Romans chapter 1 Paul taught how rejecting the Good News of God's gift of righteousness through Jesus leads to a condemned mind. In chapter 2 he goes on to explain the impossibility of being made righteous before God through obedience to the law and how it leads to self-righteousness and self-condemnation

The only way to be made righteous before God is by relying upon Jesus.

There was a time when I tried to be righteous before God and qualify for His blessings based on my obedience to the law. Instead of relying upon Jesus for my provision, I would come before the Father relying upon myself and what I had done to receive His financial blessing in my life. Instead of coming to the Father and saying, "I know You love me and will take care of me because of Jesus," I brought my own good works before the Father and said, "Father, I've been tithing and giving so I am expecting Your provision in my life." Then I would judge other people who weren't tithing and giving and disqualify them for God's provision because they weren't doing what I was doing.

As long as we focus on ourselves and what we've done or not done, we will never be truly free. The only way to live free from self-condemnation and self-righteousness is to completely rely upon Jesus and realize that you are only blessed because of Him!

Paul started in Romans 1:1-17 explaining the Good News about Jesus. He continued through the end of chapter 1 and all of chapter 2 revealing that all men are under the power of sin, and in need of a Savior. He showed us very clearly that our good works will never make us righteous before God. In chapter 3 we'll see Paul reiterate that the only way to be made righteous in God's sight and qualify for His blessing is to rely upon Jesus and His gift of righteousness. And that is the Good News about Jesus!

What is the only way to live free from self-condemnation and self-righteousness?

___

___

What did you learn today about the impossibility of relying upon your good works to be righteous and blessed by God? How will you apply what you learned to your own life?

___

___

___

Day 3

Jesus-Righteousness

Romans 3

Take time to pray before you begin.

Today we will read Romans chapter 3 and continue hearing the Good news about Jesus!

Romans 3:1-18: *1 Then what's the advantage of being a Jew? Is there any value in the ceremony of circumcision? 2 Yes, there are great benefits! First of all, the Jews were entrusted with the whole revelation of God. 3 True, some of them were unfaithful; but just because they were unfaithful, does that mean God will be unfaithful? 4 Of course not! Even if everyone else is a liar, God is true. As the Scriptures say about him, "You will be proved right in what you say, and You will win Your case in court." 5 "But," some might say, "our sinfulness serves a good purpose, for it helps people see how righteous God is. Isn't it unfair, then, for him to punish us?" (This is merely a human point of view.) 6 Of course not! If God were not entirely fair, how would he be qualified to judge the world? 7 "But," someone might still argue, "how can God condemn me as a sinner if my dishonesty highlights his truthfulness and brings him more glory?" 8 And some people even slander us by claiming that we say, "The more we sin, the better it is!" Those who say such things deserve to be condemned. 9 Well, then, should we conclude that we Jews are better than others? No, not at all, for we have already shown that all people, whether Jews or Gentiles, are under the power of sin. 10 As the scriptures say, "No one is righteous – not even one 11 No one is truly wise; no one is seeking God. 12 All have turned away; all have become useless. No one does good, not a single one." 13 "Their talk is foul, like the stench from an open grave. Their tongues are filled with lies." "Snake venom drips from their lips." 14 "Their mouths are full of cursing and bitterness." 15 "They rush to commit murder. 16 Destruction and misery always follow them. 17 They don't know where to find peace." 18 "They have no fear of God at all."*

Without Jesus, what is true of all men? Is anyone better than anyone else? (verse 9)

____

____

What truth is found in verses 10-12?

These verses reveal that all men are under the power of sin without Jesus. There is no one who is better than another person; and there is no one who is truly righteous and good in God's sight based on their good behavior. We all need a Savior! Under the law we are all disqualified for God's blessing, but because of His great love for us, Jesus came to qualify us all by giving us His gift of righteousness!

Romans 3:19-20: *19 Obviously, the law applies to those to whom it was given, for its purpose is to keep people from having excuses, and to show that the entire world is guilty before God. 20 For no one can ever be made right with God by doing what the law commands. The law simply shows us how sinful we are.*

What is the law's purpose? (verses 19-20)

What truth is the Apostle Paul revealing about the law in verse 20? What does the law show us?

The law's purpose is to show that the entire world is guilty before God because we all fail to keep it perfectly. The law is the list of things you have to do to qualify yourself for God's anointing, favor, financial blessing, or healing. The list only shows us how we don't measure up and how disqualified we are. It is impossible to ever be made righteous in God's sight by trying to obey the law because it only reveals how often we fail. But now God shows us a way to be made righteous without keeping the law.

> Romans 3:21-24: *21 But now God has shown us a way to be made right with Him without keeping the requirements of the law, as was promised in the writings of Moses and the prophets long ago. 22 We are made right with God by placing our faith in Jesus Christ. And this is true for everyone who believes, no matter who we are. 23 For everyone has sinned; we all fall short of God's glorious standard. 24 Yet God, with undeserved kindness, declares that we are righteous. He did this through Christ Jesus when he freed us from the penalty for our sins.*

How is a person made righteous apart from obeying the law? (verses 21-22)

What two things did God do for us through Jesus? (verse 24)

God showed us a different way of being declared righteous and qualified in His sight and that is through simple faith in Jesus. We don't have to pay the penalty for our sins because

Day 3

Jesus paid the penalty for us. We don't have to try and qualify ourselves because Jesus qualified us. We can give up trying and begin to trust in Jesus and the gift of righteousness He offers.

> Romans 3:25-26: *25 For God presented Jesus as the sacrifice for sin. People are made right with God when they believe that Jesus sacrificed his life, shedding His blood. This sacrifice shows that God was being fair when he held back and did not punish those who sinned in times past, 26 for he was looking ahead and including them in what he would do in this present time. God did this to demonstrate his righteousness, for he himself is fair and just, and he declares sinners to be right in his sight when they believe in Jesus.*

What wonderful Good News! God declares sinners to be righteous in His sight when they believe in Jesus!

You Are Qualified Because of Jesus!

These verses reveal very clearly that your past failures will never disqualify you for God's approval and blessing because you are free from the penalty of your sins. At the same time, your good works will never qualify you for God's approval and blessing. It is Jesus who qualifies you for God's favor, blessing, approval, wisdom, provision, healing, and guidance. No matter how many promises God has made they are all "Yes!" and "Amen!" to those who are in Christ Jesus. In Christ Jesus you qualify for them all! (2 Corinthians 1:20)

I shared with you that at one time I relied upon my good works to qualify me for God's financial provision. It was during this time that the Holy Spirit led me to Romans chapter 3 to reveal the truth that set me free from self-righteousness. I heard Jesus speak to my heart and say, "Connie, you are relying upon your own good works. You are relying upon yourself instead of Me. I made you righteous. I qualified you. Rely upon what I did for you and you will experience My provision in your life!"

At that moment, the veil of the law was removed from my eyes. I clearly saw that I could never be qualified because of anything that I had done, but that I was qualified because of what Jesus had done for me. I gave up my self-righteousness and embraced Jesus' righteousness — His gift of love to me!

Since that day, every time the devil tempts me to be condemned because of my failure, or to trust in something I did to qualify myself, I recall that "I am blessed because of Jesus. I'm qualified because Jesus made me righteous." It's a gift of His grace. I don't have to live in condemnation because of my failures, and I don't have to try to make myself righteous by my good works. I have been awakened to righteousness and live in the freedom of God's grace by being conscious, every day, that Jesus made me righteous forever the day I put my trust in Him!

> Romans 3:27: *Then what becomes of [our] pride and [our] boasting? It is excluded (banished, ruled out entirely). On what principle? [On the principle] of doing good*

deeds? No, but on the principle of faith [relying upon Jesus]. AMP [Author's Insertion]

Romans 3:27-28: *Can we boast, then, that we have done anything to be accepted by God? No, because our acquittal is not based on obeying the law. It is based on faith. 28 So we are made right with God through faith [relying upon Jesus] and not by obeying the law. [Author's Insertion] NLT*

Romans 3:29: *After all, is God the God of the Jews only? Isn't he also the God of the Gentiles? Of course he is. 30 There is only one God, and he makes people right with himself only by faith, whether they are Jews or Gentiles. 31 Well then, if we emphasize faith [relying upon Jesus] does this mean that we can forget about the law? Of course not! In fact, only when we have faith [rely upon Jesus] do we truly fulfill the law. [Author's Insertion]*

Why is our pride and our boasting about our good deeds banished entirely? (verse 27)

___

___

How do we fulfill the law? (verse 31)

___

___

In these verses, Paul explained that we have no reason to boast in anything we have done to be accepted by God. Our acquittal is not based on our obedience, but on our faith, which is relying on Jesus.

When people hear the Good News that they don't have to qualify themselves or make themselves righteous by their obedience to the law, the same question arises, "Does that mean that we can just forget about obeying God, since that is not how we are made righteous anyway?" The Apostle Paul answered this question with an emphatic, "Of course not!" The truth is that it is only when we rely upon Jesus that we truly fulfill the law. Jesus said in John 15:5, "If you abide in Me, you will bear much abundant fruit, but apart from Me you can do nothing!"

Romans 7:12 says that the law is "holy, just, and good." It's only through faith in Jesus that we can fulfill the law by being declared holy, just, and good in Christ. A person who has truly surrendered their own self-righteousness and embraced Jesus' righteousness, has the power of the Holy Spirit working in them to produce the fruit of righteousness in their life. The power to live free from sin and live a righteous life is found only in relying upon Jesus.

As long as we are focusing on the law to make us righteous, we will find ourselves living in condemnation and self-righteousness, which can only produce the vicious cycle of sin in our lives. But as we awake to our righteousness, by embracing the truth that we have been made righteous and good in Jesus, we will find ourselves living free from the power of sin. As we continue to embrace our true identity, the power of the Holy Spirit is able to produce the fruit of love, joy, peace, patience, goodness, kindness, humility, faith and self-control in our lives.

So Awake to Righteousness!

Heavenly Father, thank You for the gift of righteousness that You have given me through Jesus. I now know that my failures will never disqualify me and my good works can never qualify me for Your favor and blessing. You have qualified me for Your blessing and approval because Jesus made me righteous. I can live free from condemnation and self-righteousness simply by relying upon what You did for me. I don't have to try in my own strength anymore! You will bring the fruit of righteousness out in my life as I trust You and embrace Your gift of righteousness in Jesus. Thank You for loving me so much! Thank You for revealing to me that the true Good News is all about Jesus!

What is the main truth you learned from today's study?

Week 3

Self-Focus vs Jesus-Focus

Romans Chapter 4

Day 1

Living by Relying Upon Jesus

Day 2

The Promise of Righteousness

Day 3

Your Identity is Found in Jesus

Living by Relying Upon Jesus

Romans 4:1-8

Take time to pray before you begin.

Romans 1:17 says that the righteous shall live by faith (relying upon Jesus). But what does it mean to live by relying upon Jesus? Romans Chapter 4 gives us a very clear picture of what it looks like to live by faith in what Jesus did for us. In it we see Abraham as our example of how we are made righteous not by our works, but through faith in Jesus. I often revisit Romans 4 when I find myself being tempted to rely upon myself instead of Jesus. It helps me refocus my attention on Jesus and reminds me of what it means to rely upon Him every day.

Righteousness is not a wage to be earned, but a gift to be received

Romans 4:1-5: *1 Abraham was, humanly speaking, the founder of our Jewish nation. What did He discover about being made right with God? 2 If his good deeds had made him acceptable to God, he would have had something to boast about. But that was not God's way. 3 For the Scriptures tell us, "Abraham believed God, and God counted him as righteous because of his faith." 4 When people work, their wages are not a gift, but something they have earned. 5 But people are counted as righteous, not because of their work, but because of their faith in God who forgives sinners.*

What did Abraham discover about being made acceptable and righteous in God's sight? (verse 3)

If you have to earn righteousness through your good works, it's not a gift. What truth is revealed in verses 4-5?

Read verses 3-5 in the Message Bible: *3 What we read in Scripture is, "Abraham entered into what God was doing for him, and that was the turning point. He trusted God to set him right instead of trying to be right on his own." 4 If you're a hard worker and do a good job, you deserve your pay; we don't call your wages a gift. 5 But if you see that the job is too big for you, that it's something only God can do, and you trust him to do it – you could never do it for yourself no matter how hard and long you worked – well, that trusting-him-to-do-it is what gets you set right with God, by God. Sheer Gift.*

What was the turning point in Abraham's life? (verse 3)

I can relate to this passage of Scripture. For many years, I tried to earn God's approval through my good works. I thought it was my performance that qualified me for His blessings. My focus was continually on what I needed to do or what I was doing wrong. Self-reliance instead of depending upon Jesus produced discouragement, condemnation, pride, fear and insecurity in my heart. The turning point in my life came when I turned my focus from what I needed to do for Jesus and entered into what He had done for me. I surrendered the lie that told me I had to earn God's approval, realizing the job was too big for me and I could never be good enough by depending upon myself. All my striving to be blessed only led to frustration and disappointment which finally brought me to the end of myself so that I could truly focus on Jesus and embrace His gift of righteousness. I entered into rest because the work had already been done at the cross. You and I now stand completely righteous, perfect, approved, accepted, and qualified before our Heavenly Father, not based on anything we've done, but based on everything that Jesus has done for us.

So how do you determine if you are self-reliant? If your thoughts automatically default to what you need to do, or how you are missing the mark in order to earn God's blessings and favor, you are relying on yourself. The fruit of self-effort produces either condemnation or pride, discouragement, fear, and insecurity.

When you finally come to the place where you realize that the job is too big for you and you can never qualify yourself, you are in the place of relying on Jesus. Rest in the truth that righteousness is not something to be earned, but a gift to be received. As you rely upon what Jesus has done to make you righteous, and the promises you have in Him, you will bear the fruit of peace, joy and love.

Focusing on Jesus Produces the Fruit of Joy in Your Life

Romans 4:6-8: *6 David also spoke of this when he described the happiness of those who are declared righteous without working for it. 7 Oh, what joy for those whose disobedience is forgiven, whose sins are put out of sight. 8 Yes, what joy for those whose sin is no longer counted against them by the Lord [whose record the LORD has cleared of sin].*

Romans 4:8 in the KJV says: *Blessed is the man to whom the Lord <u>will not</u> impute sin. KJV*

When does a person truly become happy? Where does true joy come from?

With this in mind, where do you think depression comes from?

Hebrews 8:12: *"I will forgive their wickedness, and I will never again remember their sins."*

What did your Heavenly Father promise you in this verse?

What happiness a person experiences when their focus turns from themselves, to Jesus, and they realize that they are declared righteous through His good work, not by any work of their own. What joy for those who understand that the Lord no longer counts their sin against them, and their failures have been cleared from their record forever!

The words *will not* in Romans 4:8 literally mean: "a double negative, strengthening the denial; *not at all;* no, never" (G3364 Strong's; Thayer's).

This is the strongest language possible stating that those who receive forgiveness will not ever have their sins held against them. He didn't just say, "did not" or "does not," but "will not," implying that even future tense sins have been dealt with through the sacrificial offering of Jesus (Hebrews 10:10-14). Your past, present and future sins have been cleared from your record. Your Heavenly Father made a covenant promise with you through Jesus in which He says, "I will never, no never again remember your sins. I will never count your sins against you. You are free from the penalty of all your sins!"

Impute (G3049 Strong's) also means "to think upon," or "to take inventory of." Blessed is the man of whom the Lord is not taking inventory of his failures. (Romans 4:8) Happy is the man of whom the Lord is not thinking upon his sin. Instead, He's thinking upon the gift of righteousness that has been given to him in Jesus (Ephesians 1:4).

Romans 4:6-8 clearly shows us what causes depression in a person's heart. Why is depression so common in our world today? The reason is because people are focused on their failures. If you believe the lie that something is wrong with you, and you have to pay for your mistakes, shame and guilt will cause your heart to become sad and depressed.

This depression is the result of a heart believing a lie about God, themselves, or the circumstances of their life. Every time I've struggled with discouragement or sadness in my heart, it's because my focus was on my negative circumstances and failures, instead of Jesus. But every time I focus on Jesus and receive the truth that He loves me, has cleared my record of all my mistakes, and has made me perfect in His sight, I again experience pure joy in my heart.

Before Tony and I were married, I got pregnant with our oldest son. For years I believed the devil's lie that because of what I had done, I would have to pay for my mistake for the rest of my life. I believed God was imputing my sin against me. Because of my wrong thinking, we experienced lack, strife, and unhappiness in our home, and it went on for a very long time. My heart was filled with condemnation, guilt, and shame, which created the vicious cycle of sin in my life. Even though I was a Christian, I wasn't experiencing the abundant life Jesus came to give me.

When you are focused on yourself, you think thoughts like this: "This is my fault and I'm going to have to pay for it. Something is wrong with me." Depression, discouragement, condemnation, shame and guilt are the result of living your life depending on yourself.

In contrast when you are focused on Jesus, you think thoughts like this: "Jesus, You set me free from the penalty of my sin, made me righteous, and qualified me for every blessing. You rescued me when I couldn't save myself and You will do it again, rescuing me as many times as I need rescuing. Thank You for loving me so much!"

What joy I experienced when I realized that my record had been cleared, regardless of what my mistakes had been. Jesus had paid a great price to set me free, and because of that I could stand before my Heavenly Father— perfectly righteous, blameless, innocent, and without a single fault—free from guilt and shame, and all because of Jesus. When I embraced the truth, what happiness filled my heart! It felt like I had been given a death sentence for a crime I had committed, and then suddenly had all of the charges against me dropped, freeing me from my crime.

> 2 Corinthians 1:9-10: *We felt like we'd been sent to death row, that it was all over for us. As it turned out, it was the best thing that could have happened. Instead of trusting in our own strength or wits to get out of it, we were forced to trust God totally—not a bad idea since he's the God who raises the dead! And he did it, rescued us from certain doom. And he'll do it again, rescuing us as many times as we need rescuing. MSG*
>
> Isaiah 61:10: *I am overwhelmed with joy in the LORD my God! For he has dressed me with the clothing of salvation and draped me in a robe of righteousness. I am like a bridegroom in his wedding suit or a bride with her jewels.*

What did you learn today about what it means to live by relying upon Jesus? How will you apply it to your life?

____

____

____

____

____

Take some time right now to turn your focus upon Jesus and thank Him for what He has done for you!

The Promise of Righteousness

Romans 4:9-15

Take time to pray before you begin.

Today we will look at verses 9-15 of Romans chapter 4 and continue to see what it means to live by relying upon Jesus.

> Roman 4:9-15: *9 Now, is this blessing only for the Jews, or is it also for the uncircumcised Gentiles? Well, we have been saying that Abraham was counted as righteous by God because of his faith. 10 But how did this happen? Was he counted as righteous only after he was circumcised, or was it before he was circumcised? Clearly, God accepted Abraham before he was circumcised! 11 Circumcision was a sign that Abraham already had faith and that God had already accepted him and declared him to be righteous – even before he was circumcised. So Abraham is the spiritual father of those who have faith but have not been circumcised. They are counted as righteous because of their faith* ***[reliance upon Jesus]****. 12 And Abraham is also the spiritual father of those who have been circumcised, but only if they have the same kind of faith Abraham had before he was circumcised. 13 Clearly, God's promise to give the whole earth to Abraham and his descendants was based not on his obedience to God's law, but on a right relationship with God that comes by faith* ***[reliance upon Jesus]****. 14 <u>If God's promise is only for those who obey the law, then faith is not necessary and the promise is pointless.</u> 15 For the law always brings punishment on those who try to obey it. (The only way to avoid breaking the law, is to have no law to break!) [Author's Insertions in Bold]*

What was God's promise to Abraham and his descendants based on? (verse 13)

____

____

Explain in your own words the truth found in verse 14?

____

> Read Romans 4:14-15 in the Message Bible: *14 If those who get what God gives them only get it by doing everything they are told to do and filling out all the right forms properly signed, that eliminates personal trust completely and turns the promise into an ironclad contract! That's not a holy promise, that's a business deal.*

15 A contract drawn up by a hard-nosed lawyer and with plenty of fine print only makes sure that you will never be able to collect. But if there is no contract in the first place, simply a promise – and God's promise at that – you can't break it.

What completely eliminates personal trust in Jesus? What truth is revealed to you in these verses?

If you could make yourself righteous and qualify yourself for God's blessing by obeying the law, then faith in Jesus would be unnecessary, and God's promise to make you righteous in Christ would be pointless.

There are Christians who have put their faith in Christ for their eternal salvation, but then they fall back into the deception that God is going to bless them based on their performance. This is what happened to the Galatians. Paul told them that if they were going to trust in their good works to be made righteous before God, Christ had become of no benefit to them (Galatians 5:4). Likewise today, many Christians do not experience the full benefits of their salvation because they are making faith void by trusting in their own goodness. When we believe the lie that we can somehow qualify ourselves through our obedience to the law, we have stopped relying upon Jesus and begun relying upon ourselves. We have forgotten what Jesus has done for us.

Your Heavenly Father promised to make you righteous and bless you, not by you filling out all the right forms, following all the right steps, and trying to do everything right. He promised to bless you simply through your faith in Jesus. When you finally realize that the job is too big for you, and you can never qualify yourself, then you'll confidently surrender your own self-effort and truly begin to rely upon Jesus to qualify you. Jesus came to give you the gift of righteousness through your faith in Him.

Self-focused — I am qualified by my good works = condemnation or self-righteousness

Jesus-focused — I am qualified because of Jesus! = thankfulness, peace and joy

Romans 4:16: *Therefore, [inheriting] the promise is the outcome of faith and depends [entirely] on faith, in order that it might be given as an act of grace (unmerited favor), to make it stable and valid and guaranteed to all his descendants—not only to the devotees and adherents of the Law, but also to those who share the faith of Abraham, who is [thus] the father of us all. AMP*

What does inheriting the promise of righteousness depend on and who is it guaranteed to?

So why is it such Good News that a person can receive the gift of righteousness simply by relying upon Jesus? And what exactly does it means to be declared righteous in God's

Day 2

sight? Let's look at the definition of *righteousness* again:

Righteousness means: "innocent; free from guilt or blame; justified" (1342, 1343, 1344 Strong's)

> *It is the judicial act of God, by which he pardons all the sins of those who believe in Christ, and accounts, accepts, and treats them as righteous in the eye of the law.... In addition to the pardon of sin, justification declares that all the claims of the law are satisfied.... The law is not relaxed or set aside, but is declared to be fulfilled in the strictest sense; and so the person justified is declared to be entitled to all the advantages and rewards arising from perfect obedience to the law. Romans 5:1-10). It proceeds on the ... crediting to the believer by God himself of the perfect righteousness ... of Jesus Christ (Romans 10:3-9). Justification is not the forgiveness of a man without righteousness, but a declaration that he possesses a righteousness which perfectly and forever satisfies the law, namely, Christ's righteousness (2 Corinthians 5:21; Romans 4:6-8). www.christiananswers.net/dictionary/justification.html:Bible Encyclopedia*

With this definition in mind, explain in your own words why being declared righteous in Jesus is such Good News.

___

___

___

The reason the message of righteousness through Jesus is such Good News is because it is imputed through no work or effort of your own, but rather through simple faith in Jesus. You simply receive a gift that qualifies you for all the rewards and advantages of perfect obedience to the law.

So what are the rewards of perfect obedience to the law? What are the advantages of being declared righteous in Jesus?

1. Complete acceptance and approval in God's sight

   2 Corinthians 5:21: *For our sake He made Christ [virtually] to be sin Who knew no sin, so that in and through Him we might become... the righteousness of God [what we ought to be, approved and acceptable and in right relationship with Him, by His goodness]. AMP*

One of the many benefits of being declared righteous in Jesus is that you are completely approved of and accepted by your Heavenly Father, forever. Approval and acceptance is a need of every human heart. In the world's system, people are constantly seeking approval from others based on their performance. But in God's kingdom, approval and acceptance are given as a gift, through simple faith in Jesus.

2. Blessed in every area of your life

   Read Deuteronomy 28:1-13

In Deuteronomy 28:1-13, the rewards and blessings of perfect obedience to the law are listed. However, since no one, except Jesus, has ever obeyed the law perfectly, we all are disqualified from these blessings based on our performance. The Good News is these blessings are part of our inheritance because we've been given the gift of the perfect obedience of Jesus. We are not blessed because we obeyed perfectly. We are blessed because Jesus obeyed perfectly (Romans 5:19)

For a good part of my Christian life I tried to qualify myself for these blessings through my perfect obedience, but since I often failed, my own heart judged me disqualified. When I realized that Jesus gave me His righteousness as a gift, and qualified me for His blessings, my heart was filled with peace and joy, and I began to receive His blessings with a thankful heart. I knew I didn't deserve them because I did sometimes fail, but I received them as a gift of His love to me. So now when I read Deuteronomy 28:1-13, I keep Jesus in clear focus.

You and I are blessed when we come in. We are blessed when we go out. Our children are blessed. The Lord commands His blessing on the work of our hands and causes us to have a surplus of prosperity. We are the lender and not the borrower; the head and not the tail because Jesus made us righteous as a gift of His grace!

3. Prosperity

   Proverbs 13:21: *Prosperity is the reward of the righteous. NIV*

4. Health and renewed youth

   Read Isaiah 53:4-12. *Psalm 103:5 He fills my life with good things. My youth is renewed like the eagle's!*

5. Favor and guidance

   Psalm 5:12: *Surely, LORD, you bless the righteous; you surround them with your favor as with a shield. NIV*

6. Financial abundance

   Psalm 37:17,19: *17 The LORD sustains the righteous. 19 They will not be ashamed in the time of evil, and in the days of famine they will have abundance. NASB*

   2 Corinthians 9:8-11: *8 God is able to make all grace abound to you, so that in all things at all times, having all that you need, you will abound in every good work. 9 As it is written: "He has scattered abroad his gifts to the poor; their righteousness endures forever." 10 Now he who supplies seed to the sower and bread for food will also supply and increase your store of seed and will enlarge the harvest of your righteousness. 11 You will be enriched in every way so that you can be generous on every occasion. NIV*

Another benefit of being declared righteous is that the Scriptures say that during the time of a bad economy, the righteous will enjoy abundance. All grace abounds toward the righteous and the Lord provides their needs with plenty left over to be a blessing to others.

When I hear bad news about the economy, I remember that Jesus made me righteous and qualified me for these promises in my life. Instead of focusing on myself and becoming fearful and worried, I turn my focus to Jesus and ask for His grace to continue to trust Him and what He says about me and my family. He says in Psalm 37:19 that in the time of famine the righteous will prosper. When you rely upon Jesus, you will experience His peace and abundant blessing in your life.

7. Deliverance and victory in every situation

   Psalm 34:15,17,19: *15 The eyes of the LORD are on the righteous and his ears are attentive to their cry... 17 The righteous cry out, and the LORD hears them; he delivers them from all their troubles. 19 The righteous person may have many troubles, but the LORD DELIVERS HIM FROM THEM ALL. NIV*

8. A joyful and peaceful heart and home

   Proverbs 3:33: *The Lord declares blessed (joyful and favored with blessings) the home of the righteous. AMP Isaiah 32:17-18 And the effect of righteousness will be peace [internal and external], and the result of righteousness will be quietness and confident trust forever. 18 My people shall dwell in a peaceable habitation, in safe dwellings, and in quiet resting places. AMP*

9. Children who live in the truth and have great peace

   Proverbs 11:21: *[The] seed of the righteous shall be delivered. KJV*

   Psalm 103:17:*His righteousness is to your children's children—*

   Isaiah 54:13 *I will teach all your children, and they will enjoy great peace.*

   Psalm 112:2-3 *Their children will be successful everywhere; an entire generation of godly people will be blessed. 3 Prosperity and welfare are in his house, and his righteousness endures forever.* Proverbs 31:28: *Her children rise up and call her blessed (happy, fortunate, and to be envied)*

10. False accusation against you will not prosper

    Isaiah 54:17: *But no weapon that is formed against you shall prosper, and every tongue that shall rise against you in judgment you shall show to be in the wrong. This [peace, righteousness, security, triumph over opposition] is the heritage of the servants of the Lord [those in whom the ideal Servant of the Lord is reproduced]; this is the righteousness or the vindication which they obtain from Me [this is that which I impart to them as their justification], says the Lord. AMP*

11. Powerful and effective prayers

    Proverbs 10:24: *The desire of the righteous shall be granted. KJV; James 5:16: The prayer of a righteous man is powerful and effective. NIV (1 John 5:14,15)*

12. Protection: Psalm 91

Proverbs 12:21: *No [actual] evil, misfortune, or calamity shall come upon the righteous. AMP*

These Scriptures reveal some of the rewards and advantages of being declared righteous in God's sight through Jesus. You don't have to try to be good enough to earn them—they are a pure gift of God's grace. They describe who you are and what you have in Jesus. They give you a clear picture of what it means to be declared righteous in Him. When you face difficult circumstances in your life, focus your attention on Jesus, and remember that He qualified you for each one of these promises. When you read these Scriptures in the Bible, keep in mind that they are your inheritance in Christ, not because of what you've done, but because of what Jesus has done for you. When you live by relying upon Jesus and not yourself, you'll experience joy and peace in this world no matter what challenges life brings.

What did you learn today about what it means to be declared righteous in Jesus? Why is the gift of righteousness such Good News?

Your Identity is Found in Jesus

Romans 4:17-24

Take time to pray before you begin.

Today we will take a look at Romans 4:17-24 and finish up our study of what it means to live by relying upon Jesus. In these verses we will discover that we are not defined by our past mistakes nor our present circumstances. Our identity is found only in what our Heavenly Father declares about us in Christ.

> Romans: 4:17-21: *17 As it is written, I have made you the father of many nations. **[He was appointed our father]** in the sight of God in Whom he believed, Who gives life to the dead and speaks of the nonexistent things as if they [already] existed.*
> *18 [For Abraham, human reason for] hope being gone, hoped in faith that he should become the father of many nations, as he had been promised, so [numberless] shall your descendants be. 19 He did not weaken in faith when he considered the [utter] impotence of his own body, which was as good as dead because he was about a hundred years old, or [when he considered] the barrenness of Sarah's [deadened] womb. 20 No unbelief or distrust made him waver (doubtingly question) concerning the promise of God, but he grew strong and was empowered by faith as he gave praise and glory to God, 21 fully satisfied and assured that God was able and mighty to keep His word and to do what He had promised. AMP*

What did the Father declare about Abraham? What did God see when He looked at him? (verse 17)

Even though Abraham's circumstances looked hopeless, what did he hope for? (verse 18)

What negative circumstances was Abraham facing? (verse 19)

Did his negative circumstances cause him to doubt what the Father had declared about him? How did he respond to his Heavenly Father? (verses 20-21)

Day 3

The Father said to Abraham, "I've made you the father of many nations—the father of those who will rely upon Jesus for their righteousness," but Abraham's circumstances looked hopeless. He was childless, and His body was old and his wife was barren. What the Father said about Abraham did not look true. Yet, Abraham made a choice not to allow his weaknesses or his present circumstances to define him. When he considered his situation, he did not doubtingly question his Father's promise to him. Instead he was empowered by faith as he gave praise and glory to God. His heart was fully persuaded that whatever the Father said about him, He was able to perform in his life.

The same is true of you. Your Heavenly Father looks at you and declares you righteous in Jesus. He speaks through His word and says: (put your name on the lines below)

____________________, you are completely accepted, approved and without fault in my sight. You are qualified for all of My blessings because of Jesus: 2 Corinthians 5:21; Ephesians 1:4

____________________, My Spirit lives within you and I will bring out the fruit of righteousness in your life: Galatians 5:22-23

____________________, I command my blessings upon every area of your life. You are anointed and empowered to prosper in Christ: Deuteronomy 28:1-13; Ephesians 1:3

____________________, by the stripes of Jesus, you are healed. Your youth is renewed like the eagle's: Isaiah 53:4,5; Psalm 103:5

____________________, you are surrounded with my favor as a shield: Psalm 5:12

____________________, My grace abounds toward you and you have more than enough to give to every good work. In the time of famine, you will enjoy abundance: 2 Corinthians 9:8; Psalm 37:19

____________________, I hear your prayers and I will rescue you and deliver you from all your troubles. You are an overcomer in Jesus: Psalm 34:19; Romans 8:37

____________________, I declare your home joyful and favored with blessings. Your home is blessed with peace: Proverbs 3:33; Isaiah 32:17-18

____________________, I will rescue your children. I will teach them and give them great peace. They are mighty and blessed upon the earth. They shall rise up and call you blessed: Proverbs 11:21; Isaiah 54:13; Psalm 112:2-3; Proverbs 31:28

Just like Abraham, your circumstances may not look like what God says is true. Are you facing a situation in your life right now that does not look like what the Father says about you in Christ?

____

____

This is the time you decide who you really are on the inside. What is true about you? Are you defined by your circumstances or are you defined by what your Father says about you in Christ? The truth is: it doesn't matter what it looks like. If your Heavenly Father says you're righteous in Jesus; if He declares your home joyful and blessed with peace; if He says you're favored, healed, prosperous, and blessed; if He says your children are mighty and blessed upon the earth, obedient to His will, and great is their peace; if He says they rise up and call you blessed, then that's exactly what is true about you, despite your circumstances. You are not defined by your past mistakes, nor are you defined by your present circumstances. You are defined by what your Heavenly Father says about you in Christ.

Romans 4:20 says that Abraham was empowered by faith as he gave praise and glory to God. Abraham was fully convinced that what God had promised He was also able to perform. One definition of the Greek word for *glory* is "the Father's good opinion." *(Vine's New Testament).* 2 Corinthians 1:20 says we give glory to God when we say "amen" to every promise we have in Jesus. Abraham glorified God by agreeing with the Father's good opinion of himself. He gave praise and glory to God by saying, "Father, if You say I'm the father of many nations, then that's who I am no matter what my circumstances look like. Thank you for blessing me and my children by making us righteous through faith in Jesus!" That's what it means to give glory to God. That's what it looks like to live by relying upon Jesus – you agree with the Father's good opinion of you in Christ.

> Romans 4:19-21: *19 Abraham didn't focus on his own impotence and say, "It's hopeless. This hundred-year-old body could never father a child." Nor did he survey Sarah's decades of infertility and give up. 20 He didn't tiptoe around God's promise, asking cautiously skeptical questions. He plunged into the promise and came up strong, ready for God, 21 sure that God would make good on what He had said. MSG*

Where was Abraham's focus? How did he respond to God's promise?

____

____

Asking skeptical questions about what your Heavenly Father says about you in Christ will keep you in bondage to your past mistakes and your present circumstances. I used to tiptoe around God's promises, asking cautiously skeptical questions such as, "Well if what God says is true about me then why am I experiencing the exact opposite?" "If God says I have abundance, then why do I constantly struggle to get by?" "If God's promise is true then why did that person die?" This constant questioning of God's promises only served to create doubt and discouragement in my heart. Even though I heard the promises of God, my heart responded by saying, "Look at my life! That just can't be true about me." I put more value in my opinion of myself and my situation than in my Father's opinion of me. They were lies of the devil that were actually intended to get me to embrace the ultimate lie, "God cannot be trusted. And what He says about Himself and about me is not true."

The turning point in my life came when I gave up my own opinion of myself and began embracing my Father's view of me in Christ. I asked Jesus to help me believe who He says that I am in Him, and then I began glorifying God by agreeing with everything my Father says, no matter what the circumstances looked like. No longer defined by my past mistakes or present circumstances, I embraced my true identity in Christ. As a result, I began to experience favor, blessing, and the fruit of righteousness in my life. As I continued to live by relying upon Jesus and agreeing with what my Father declared about me, my whole life was transformed from the inside out.

Tiptoeing around God's promises, asking cautiously skeptical questions, will only serve to keep you in a self-focused, condemned, shame-filled, discouraged life. What our Heavenly Father says about us is true! We are abundantly blessed! We are healed! We are perfect and holy and righteous in God's sight because of Jesus! So let's live our lives glorifying our Father God. Let's live by relying upon Jesus! When we face negative circumstances in our lives, let's turn to our loving Father and say, "Father, what do You say about this situation in my life? Remind me who I am one more time." Then listen as He speaks His words of truth to your heart, and respond by agreeing with Him, "Father, what You say about me is what defines me, not my circumstances. I am who You say I am in Christ. Thank You for loving me!"

Self-focused: I am defined by my weaknesses and failures

Jesus-focused: My identity is found in Jesus and my new nature in Him

Self-focused: What God says is not true about me, just look at my circumstances. If God's promise is true than why am I experiencing this? I am defined by my present circumstances.

Jesus-focused: What my Father says about me is true no matter what I see. My identity is found in Jesus, and the promises I have in Him. I will see the glory of the Lord in my life!

Let's finish Romans chapter 4 by reading verses 22-25: 22 *That is why his faith was credited to him as righteousness (right standing with God). 23 But [the words], It was credited to him, were written not for his sake alone, 24 but [they were written] for our sakes too. [Righteousness, standing acceptable and approved before God] will be granted and credited to us also who believe in (trust in, adhere to, and rely on) God, who raised Jesus our Lord from the dead. 25 Who was betrayed and put to death because of our misdeeds and was raised to secure our justification (our acquittal), [making our account balance and absolving us from all guilt before God]. AMP*

When you trust in Jesus, what is granted and credited to you? (verse 24)

Day 3

Why was Jesus put to death? (verse 25)

Why was Jesus raised from the dead? (verse 25)

Jesus was betrayed and put to death to free us from the penalty of our sins, completely freeing us from all guilt before God. He rose again to secure our righteousness forever. We are not defined by our past mistakes nor our present circumstances. We are defined by what our Heavenly Father says about us in Christ.

This same story is revealed throughout the whole Bible. God spoke to men and told them what He saw in them despite their weaknesses and negative circumstances. When a person chose to believe what God said, the glory of the Lord manifested in their lives. Each one lived by relying upon Jesus. They turned their focus from themselves to Jesus and agreed with what the Father said about them.

> Abraham: His circumstances said that he was old and his wife was barren, but the Father said he was a righteous father of many nations.
>
> Gideon: His circumstances said that his clan was the weakest in the country, but the Father said he was a mighty man of valor.
>
> Saul: He was a murderer, but the Father saw him as the great Apostle Paul.
>
> David: He was a murderer and an adulterer, but the Father saw a great king.
>
> Moses: He was a murderer and a stutterer; but the Father saw a great leader who would deliver his people.
>
> Esther: She was a poor Jewish girl, but the Father saw a great queen.
>
> Peter: He denied Jesus three times, but the Father saw him as a man of faith.

When we begin to truly rely upon Jesus and agree with our Father, just like Abraham, we will experience His glory (His good opinion of us) in our lives.

These are examples of the Father's great love for us all! He looks at each one of us through the eyes of love and declares things we cannot see. When we begin to truly rely upon Jesus and agree with our Father, just like Abraham, we will experience His glory (His good opinion of us) in our lives. He died to set us free from the guilt and shame of our failures. He rose again to secure our righteousness! We are qualified forever in Jesus! All that is left for us to do is thankfully acknowledge this gift He has lovingly given to all of us in Jesus!

So Awake to Righteousness!

Thank You Father, for revealing to me that my past mistakes and my present circumstances do not define who I am. My true identity is found in what You say about me in Christ. Give me the grace to believe what You say no matter what I see. Help me live my life completely relying upon what Jesus did for me. I give up my skeptical questions about Your promises, and I choose today to agree with everything You say about me in Jesus. I am diving right in and I know I will come up strong because You are well able to do what You have promised in my life. I love You, Father, because You first loved me!

What did you learn this week about the difference between being self-focused and Jesus-focused? What did you learn from Abraham's life about what it means to live your life by completely relying upon Jesus?

Week 4

The Benefits of Being Made Righteous

Romans 5:1-11

Day 1

Peace with God

Day 2

Access to God's Grace

Day 3

Secure in God's Love

This week we will take a look at Romans chapter 5, which naturally falls into two parts. In the first eleven verses the Apostle Paul explains the benefits of being declared righteous through faith in Christ. This will be the focus of Week 4.

The second part of Romans chapter 5, verses 12-21, contrasts the difference between Adam's sin, which brought condemnation to all men, and Jesus' death and resurrection, which brought the gift of righteousness and life to all who will receive it. This will be the focus of Week 5.

Peace with God

Romans 5:1

Take time to pray before you begin.

As we continue reading through Romans, keep in mind that this book was written as a letter and wasn't broken into the chapters that we see today. We will begin in Romans 5 and then go back and read the last two verses of Romans 4 to get a clear picture of the truth being taught.

Romans 5:1 says: *Therefore, since we have been made right in God's sight by faith, we have peace with God because of what Jesus Christ our Lord has done for us. NLT*

What benefit of being righteous through Jesus is revealed in this verse?

____

____

Why do you and I have peace with God?

____

____

This verse says that because we've been made righteous in God's sight through faith in Jesus, we now have peace with God because of what Jesus did for us.

So what did Jesus do for us? Let's back up to the previous chapter and read Romans 4:23-25 to get a clear understanding of the answer to this question.

Romans 4:23-25: *23 And when God counted him as righteous, it wasn't just for Abraham's benefit. It was recorded 24 for our benefit, too, assuring us that God will also count us as righteous if we believe in him, the One who raised Jesus our Lord from the dead. 25 He was handed over to die because of our sins, and He was raised to life to make us right with God. NLT*

Romans 4:25 in the Amplified Bible says, *"Who was betrayed and put to death because of our misdeeds and was raised to secure our justification (our acquittal), [making our account balance and absolutely absolving us from all guilt before God].*

Why was Jesus put to death? (verse 25)

____

____

Why was Jesus raised from the dead? (verse 25)

____

____

Jesus died to set us free from the penalty of our sin which is condemnation. His death freed us from all the shame associated with our failures and absolutely absolved us of all guilt before God. He rose again to secure our righteousness forever, qualifying us for every promised blessing of God. Because of what Jesus did for us, we have perfect peace with God.

The word *peace* in Romans 5:1 comes from the Greek word *eipnvn* (G1515). According to the Strong's Concordance it means: "(to join); prosperity; one; rest, to set at one again."

According to the practical word studies in the New Testament this word peace means: "to be bound, joined with God as one." It means "assured, confident, and secure in the love and care of God."

According to Romans 5:1, the first benefit of being made righteous by faith in Jesus is peace with God. When God gave you His perfect righteousness as a gift, you actually became one with Him. When you live conscious of this truth, you live with an abiding peace in your soul. You live confident and secure in the love and care that He has for you. Peace is the result of relating to God based on what Jesus did for us instead of what we do for Him. Those who believe they are separate from God and think they have to perform up to a certain standard to be pleasing to Him will never experience true peace. They will always wonder if they are "good enough" to really be taken care of and loved by Him.

In the Garden of Eden, God gave Adam and Eve two choices:

1. They could eat of the tree of life and live as one with their Father by embracing their true identity which was based on their Father's good opinion of them.
2. They could eat of the tree of the knowledge of good and evil and judge for themselves who they were, based on their good or bad behavior.

Adam and Eve chose to eat from the fruit of their own judgment. That choice separated them from their Father and, just as God had warned, brought death and condemnation to their hearts. Spiritual death is separation from God.

The Good News of the Gospel is that Jesus came to redeem and reconcile us back to our true origin. Through simple faith in His finished work, we become one again with our Father God, never to be separated again. The moment you trust in Jesus, He declares you righteous, never to change His mind. You now have perfect peace with God forever!

This peace comes by realizing that your Father God declares you righteous and has made you one with Himself, changing the way you respond when you encounter trials in your life. As you awake to your identity in Christ, you won't fear news about the economy, your children's bad choices, or somebody's negative opinion. Jesus did something to change the way you live. You are a child of the King, loved and adored by your Father. He came so that you could live, confident and secure in your Heavenly Father's love and care, no matter what trial life might bring your way.

> Psalm 112:6-8: *6 Those who are righteous will be long remembered. 7 They do not fear bad news; they confidently trust the LORD to care of them. 8 They are confident and fearless and can face their foes triumphantly.*

How do those who understand they are righteous in Jesus respond to bad news?

We look at life's troubles differently when we embrace the truth that we are righteous in Jesus. Fear is the by-product of being unrighteous or sin-conscious, but peace with God is the fruit of being righteous-conscious.

When you live unrighteous- or sin-conscious, you live thinking you are separate from God, and those thoughts produce death — shame, guilt, and condemnation — in your heart. You live thinking something is wrong with you and that produces fear in your heart when you encounter trials. Fearful thoughts such as, "Did God bring this trial on me? Is God mad at me? Is He trying to teach me something? Will He really take care of me?" fill your head. But these fearful kind of thoughts disappear when you understand that you have peace with God. The Father's good opinion of you never changes, and He's not angry with you anymore. He promised He would never be angry and punish you again.

> Isaiah 54:9-10: *"This exile is just like the days of Noah for me. I promised then that the waters of Noah would never again flood the earth. I'm promising now no more anger. No more dressing you down. MSG 9 I swear that I will never again be angry and punish you. NLT 10 For even if the mountains walk away and the hills fall to pieces, my love won't walk away from you. My covenant commitment of peace won't fall apart." The God who has compassion on you says so. MSG*

What did God promise you in this verse?

Why does this truth bring you peace?

In these verses, God speaks of the New Covenant He has made with man through Jesus. Anyone who teaches that God is angry and punishing people for their sins is calling God a liar, because He promised in Isaiah 54:9-10, "I will never be angry and punish you again! My covenant of peace will never depart from you. I will always love you and have compassion on you!"

Isaiah 54:14 goes on to say that you shall become established in righteousness, and the thought of oppression and fear will not come near you. Fear will no longer control your life as you embrace the truth that you are one with God. When you are established in righteousness, those oppressive, lying thoughts such as, "This is my fault." "I have to pay." "What am I going to do?" "What if God doesn't come through for me?" are replaced by "Lord, You freed me from all guilt and shame, and You qualified me for Your salvation by making me righteous. I have peace with You, Father. I know that You love me, and You will work this out for my good!"

Unrighteous or **sin-conscious** = I am separate from God. His opinion of me changes based on my behavior = **fear**

Righteous-conscious = I am one with God. His good opinion of me never changes because of Jesus = **peace**

Because you have been made righteous through Jesus, you have peace with God. You don't ever have to wonder about His opinion of you during trials. He views you as forgiven, good, and qualified in Jesus because you are one with Him. Rest safe and secure in His love and care for you, and watch as He demonstrates His salvation in your life!

Why is having peace with God such Good News? How does it change the way you respond when you encounter trials ?

____

____

____

____

____

____

____

____

____

____

Access to God's Grace

Romans 5:2-5

Take time to pray before you begin.

In Day 1 of this week you learned that the first benefit of being made righteous through Jesus is peace with God. Roman 5:2 reveals the second benefit, which is access into the grace of God.

> Romans 5:2: *Through Him also we have [our] access . . . by faith into this grace (state of God's favor) in which we [firmly and safely] stand. And let us rejoice and exult in our hope of experiencing and enjoying the glory of God. AMP*
>
> Romans 5:3: *We can rejoice, too, when we run into problems and trials, for we know that they help us develop endurance.*
>
> Romans 5:4: *And endurance develops strength of character, and character strengthens our confident hope of salvation.*
>
> Romans 5:5: *And this hope will not lead to disappointment. For we know how dearly God loves us, because he has given us the Holy Spirit to fill our hearts with his love. NLT*

Through faith in Jesus what do we have access to? (verse 2)

____

____

Because we safely stand in the grace of God, what can we rejoice in? (verse 2)

____

____

Why can we rejoice when we encounter problems in life? (verse 3 and 4)

____

____

When we put our hope in the salvation we have in Jesus, what will it never lead to? Why? (verse 5)

____

____

Through Jesus we have access into this grace (state of God's favor) in which we firmly and safely stand. This grace causes us to rejoice in our hope of enjoying and experiencing the glory of God.

In order to understand the power of the truth found in these verses, let's define the words GRACE, HOPE, THE GLORY OF GOD, and SALVATION:

> **Grace:** especially the divine influence upon the heart, and its reflection in the life; acceptable, favor, gift, joy, liberality, pleasure (G5463 Strong's)
>
> **Hope:** expectation or confidence; a confident expectation of good (G1680 Strong's)
>
> **Glory of God:** primarily signifies an opinion, the honor resulting from a good opinion. It is used of the nature and acts of God in self-manifestation, i.e., what He essentially is and does (G1391 Strong's; Vine's)
>
> **Salvation:** the present experience of God's power to deliver from the bondage of sin, inclusively, to sum up all the blessings bestowed by God on men in Christ through the Holy Spirit (G4991 Strong's; Vines)

Grace is the unmerited favor and power of the Holy Spirit by which He influences your heart and manifests God's promise in your life. I know in my life when I encounter trials, or lying thoughts are filling up my head, the first thing I remember is the truth that because I've been made righteous through Jesus, I have access to the grace of God. I don't have to try to battle these doubts on my own. I have learned to look to Jesus and say, "Lord, I need your grace right now! Strengthen me by Your grace." When I am weak, His grace makes me strong! It is the power of the Holy Spirit of Grace that gives you the power to believe what your Heavenly Father says about you in the midst of a negative situation.

Because we have access to the power and unmerited favor of God, our hearts can rejoice in our hope (confident expectation) of enjoying and experiencing the glory of God. The glory of God is the Father's good opinion of you because you are one with Him. It is the manifestation of who God is and what He does. He is your Strength, Healer, Provider, Deliverer, Protector, Righteousness, Peace and Victory. Because you are one with Him, His good opinion of you is that you are strong, healed, delivered, abundantly blessed, protected, righteous, peaceful and victorious in Jesus. When you enjoy the glory of God, you experience the manifestation of who God is and who you are in Jesus in every situation!

Romans 5:3-5 says that our access to the grace of God causes our hearts to rejoice when we run into problems, because grace gives us a confident hope of salvation. Now remember, salvation is not only a ticket to heaven, but it is also God delivering you from the guilt and condemnation of your sins and bestowing on you all the blessings that are yours in Jesus, so that you can enjoy this life here on earth. Salvation is the manifestation of all the blessings you have in Christ: the manifestation of healing and health; the manifestation of favor and wisdom; the manifestation of financial provision and abundance; the manifestation

Day 2

of peace and joy; the manifestation of your children living in the truth; the manifestation of peace in your home. That's what salvation is. It's the Holy Spirit manifesting what God says about you and your situation, because of Jesus.

Trial or problem	Your Father's Good Opinion of You: His Glory and Salvation
Financial trouble	Abundantly blessed in Christ (2 Corinthians 9:8)
Sickness	Divine Health in Christ (Isaiah 53:4-5)
Trouble with your children	He gives your children great peace (Isaiah 54:13)
People saying evil things about you	Vindication is your inheritance in Christ (Isaiah 54:17)
Friends betraying or rejecting you	Acceptance and approval in Christ (Ephesians 1:6)
Decisions to make	You are led by God's Spirit (Romans 8:14)
Strife or depression in your home	Joy and peace in your home (Proverbs 3:33; Isaiah 32:17-19)
Temptation or trial	God delivers the righteous from all their troubles (Psalm 34:17-19)

Romans 5:5 says that this confident hope of salvation in Jesus will never disappoint because we know how much the Father loves us. I have found that every time I've been disappointed, it was because I had my hope in something other than Jesus. It didn't matter whether it was a friend, my husband, my children, a business, a time frame or just my expectation of how God should fulfill His promise to me. Anytime I prayed for something that didn't work out the way I had hoped it would, it created great disappointment in my heart.

For example: One time my husband Tony and I agreed in prayer for a particular job to provide for our family. We knew that God had promised to provide all our needs and we believed this job was the way He was going to fulfill that promise to us. When the job did not come through, we both felt like God had failed us and we were very disappointed. When I took my heart to Jesus concerning this situation, He showed me that my hope had been in the way in which I wanted the promise to be fulfilled. The job had been my provision, not Jesus. After talking to Jesus, I realized that when I put my hope in Him alone, I can rest in the truth that He knows the way and the timing that is best for me and my family.

When I redirected my hope from the job to Jesus and rested in the truth that He is my provision, I was able to see Him provide for us in a completely different way. It ended up so much better than the job we had originally put our hope in. Looking back, I am so thankful that God's provision didn't come the way we had wanted it to; our Father God had a much better plan to superabundantly bless our family. The same is true for you. Don't look to a person, or a way for Jesus to fulfill His promise to you. Rest, knowing that when you place your hope in Jesus, you will never be disappointed. He dearly loves you, and He is working everything out for your good.

Because I have access to the grace of God, I have a confident expectation of enjoying and experiencing the glory of God in every area of my life. I have put my hope in Jesus, and He has strengthened me in my darkest times. He brought me out of lack, and brought me into abundance. He's healed my body, healed my heart, healed my marriage, and blessed my children. I have seen God's salvation and experienced His glory in my life. When I have placed my hope in Jesus, I have never been disappointed!

The reason why so many other people have been disappointed in their circumstances is because they've quit hoping in Jesus. They have given up their hope in the Father's good opinion of them in Christ. They may be holding on to that heaven ticket, but they've given up the hope of seeing His salvation in the circumstances of their lives. You don't have to live that way. You can live every day in confident expectation of enjoying the glory of God because you have access to the grace of God through Jesus. His grace empowers and strengthens you to believe Him in the midst of every problem you face. And His grace manifests His good opinion of you in every area of your life.

The second benefit of being made righteous in Jesus is that you have access to the grace of God. Are you facing a particular problem or trial in your life right now?

___

___

___

Through Jesus you have access to the grace of God. How does believing this cause you to respond to the problem you are facing?

___

___

What can you put your confident expectation in without any fear of disappointment?

___

___

___

Secure in God's Love

Romans 5:5-11

Take time to pray before you begin.

Today we will look at Romans 5:5-11, and discover that the third benefit of being made righteous through faith in Jesus, is living securely in His love.

> Romans 5:5: *And this hope will not lead to disappointment. For we know how dearly God loves us, because He has given us the Holy Spirit to fill our hearts with his love. NLT*
>
> *6 While we were yet in weakness [powerless to help ourselves], at the fitting time Christ died for... the ungodly.*
>
> *7 Now it is an extraordinary thing for one to give his life even for an upright man, though perhaps for a noble and lovable and generous benefactor someone might even dare to die.*
>
> *8 But God shows and <u>clearly proves His [own] love for us</u> by the fact that while we were still sinners, Christ (the Messiah, the Anointed One) died for us.*
>
> *9 Therefore, since we are now justified (acquitted, made righteous and brought into right relationship with God) by Christ's blood, how much more [certain is it that] we shall be saved by Him from the indignation and wrath of God.*
>
> *10 For if while we were enemies we were reconciled to God through the death of His Son, it is much more [certain], now that we are reconciled, that we shall be saved (daily delivered from sin's dominion) through His resurrection life.*
>
> *11 Not only so, but we also rejoice and exultingly glory in God [in His love and perfection] through our Lord, Jesus Christ, through Whom we have now received and enjoy our reconciliation. AMP*

How did God show and clearly prove to you how much He loves you?

(Verse 8)

____

(Verse 9)

____

____

These verses clearly show us how dearly our Father loves us. He proved His love by sending Jesus to die for our sin and making us righteous in His sight through our faith in Him. The third benefit of being made righteous that is revealed in this passage of Scripture is that we can live in the security of our Heavenly Father's love, knowing He loves us unconditionally. He doesn't love you more when you do good things, nor does He love you less when you do something bad. He loved you completely when you were a sinner. When you were helpless to ever make yourself righteous, He proved His love for you by laying His very life down in exchange for yours. He took away your sin and shame and gave you the gift of His perfect righteousness. Now you stand before Him perfectly innocent, without fault, holy, and qualified not because of your good works, but because of your faith in the finished work of Jesus! That is *agape* love!

> Read Jude 1:24: *Now to Him Who is able to keep you without stumbling or slipping or falling, and to present [you] unblemished (blameless and faultless) before the presence of His glory in triumphant joy and exultation [with unspeakable, ecstatic delight]. AMP*

Because of His finished work on the cross, how does Jesus present you before the Father?

____

____

How does His heart feel about you?

____

The Father loves you so much that He sent His son to reconcile you back into His favor so that He could be one with you and enjoy an intimate, personal relationship. You are the delight of His heart. Your sins caused you to run and hide from God, but Jesus took care of your sins by completely obliterating them on the cross. Now the Father has no more consciousness of your sin (Hebrews 8:12). He only sees perfection when He looks at you. He forever proved His love by making you righteous in His sight through Jesus! Jesus presents you before the Father blameless and without fault in His sight. They are ecstatic about you!

When I received the understanding that Jesus made me righteous as a gift of His grace, and realized that I no longer had to strive to earn God's favor and blessing, the revelation of His love overwhelmed me. I realized He gave me a brand new identity in Jesus and I could now rest, safe and secure in His great love for me.

In the past when I would go through a difficult time or something bad would happen to me, I would question God's love for me because I didn't understand what Jesus really accomplished for me on the cross. Now when I face trials in my life, I turn my thoughts to my Heavenly Father and say, "Father, I know You love me because You made me righteous in Jesus!" I am free to share my most intimate thoughts and feelings with Him because I know His good opinion of me never changes. This gives me a confident hope of His salvation in my life, and brings peace and rest to my soul.

You never have to wonder again whether your Heavenly Father loves you. He proved it by giving you His gift of righteousness. Why do you know He dearly loves you? **Because He made you righteous!** Why did **He make you righteous?** Because He loves you!

And He doesn't love me any more than He loves you, nor does He love you any more than He loves me. He sent His Son for each one of us; to do the very same thing for each one of us. And it's for "whosoever will" embrace this gift of righteousness, and whosoever will let the peace and joy and security that is found in Christ, reign in their hearts.

So, let me ask you again, how do you know that your Heavenly Father loves you?

___

And why did He make you righteous?

___

You can either be unrighteous-conscious and live in the victim/death cycle, or you can be righteous-conscious and live in the victorious/life cycle

> **The Victim/Death Cycle [Unrighteous-conscious]:** Why do you feel like your Father doesn't love you? "Because of the circumstances I'm facing." Why do you think you are facing these circumstances? "Because my Father must not love me."
>
> **The Victorious/Life Cycle: [Righteous-conscious]:** How do you know your Father loves you? "Because He made me righteous!" Why did He make you righteous? "Because He loves me!"

Now let's look at Romans 5:10-11 again.

> *10 For if while we were enemies we were reconciled to God through the death of His Son, it is much more [certain], now that we are reconciled, that we shall be saved (daily delivered from sin's dominion) through His resurrection life.*
>
> *11 Not only so, but we also rejoice and exultingly glory in God [in His love and perfection] through our Lord, Jesus Christ, through whom we have now received and enjoy our reconciliation. AMP*

Now that you are reconciled through the death of Jesus, what can you be certain of? (Verse 10)

___

___

What can you rejoice in? (Verse 11)

___

___

This scripture says that God made you one with Him by giving you His perfect righteousness, through Jesus, while you were still a sinner. How much more is He going to move powerfully on your behalf, and bring forth the manifestation of His glory in your life, now that you are righteous? If He proved His love for you while you were still a sinner, how much more is He going to continue demonstrating His love for you now that you are righteous?

This is what Paul is saying in these verses. "Listen to me, you beloved righteous people of God! Wake up to who you are! You are dearly loved by the Father. He daily delivers you from the dominion of sin and frees you from all guilt and shame by reminding you of who you are in Jesus! You are wonderful. He sees you as perfect and good and innocent. You are qualified, favored, and abundantly blessed because of Jesus! You can rejoice in His love and perfection and enjoy an intimate, loving, authentic relationship with Him because He reconciled you to Himself. You've been made one with the Father. You've been made one with Jesus. Whatever the Father says about Himself, that's the same good opinion He has of you, and His good opinion of you will never change!"

Since we've been made righteous through faith in Jesus, we have peace with God. We stand secure in His grace. We know how dearly our Father loves us and we confidently expect His salvation in every area of our lives. Why? Because He loves us! How do we know He loves us? Because He made us righteous! Why did He make us righteous? Because He loves us! This is what it means to awake to righteousness!

According to Romans 5:1-11, what are the three benefits of being made righteous through faith in Jesus?

____

____

____

How does this change the way you relate to your Heavenly Father?

____

____

____

So Awake to Righteousness!

Heavenly Father: I now realize that because I've been made righteous through faith in Jesus, I have peace with You. I am one with You and I never have to be afraid that You will be angry with me. When I am weak, You make me strong! I am confident and secure in Your great love for me. Thank You for Your gift of righteousness!

Reigning in Life Through Jesus

Romans 5:10-21

Day 1

Condemnation vs Righteousness

Day 2

What Does It Mean to Reign in Life?

Day 3

Grace Reigns Through Righteousness

Day 1

Condemnation vs Righteousness

Romans 5:10-17

Take time to pray before you begin.

Today we are going to finish Romans chapter 5 and answer the question, "What does it mean to reign as a king in this life through Jesus Christ?" When you understand what it means, you will really start ruling and reigning in this life.

> Romans 5:10-11: *10 For if while we were enemies we were reconciled to God through the death of His Son, it is much more [certain], now that we are reconciled, that we shall be saved (daily delivered from sin's dominion) through His [resurrection] life. 11 Not only so, but we also rejoice and exultingly glory in God [in His love and perfection] through our Lord Jesus Christ, through Whom we have now received and enjoy [our] reconciliation. AMP*

Sin's Dominion is Condemnation

Sin dominates our lives through condemnation, guilt and shame. Simply put, condemnation is a negative opinion about yourself. It brings death because it causes us to feel badly about ourselves and as a result, feel separated from God. That is the power that sin has over each of our lives. No one is immune from these condemning, negative thoughts; they come to all of us.

Jesus made a way for us to finally be free from the negative, condemning opinions we have of ourselves that keep us in that vicious cycle of sin. While you were still a sinner and utterly helpless to save yourself, Jesus came and rescued you from sin's power by making you righteous. Now that you are perfect, holy, and favored in God's sight, how much more will He daily deliver you from sin's dominion (condemnation, shame, and guilt) through His resurrection life?

Because we have been set free from sin's dominion (condemnation, shame, and guilt) we now can rejoice and exultingly glory in the Father's good opinion of us. We are free to receive His unconditional love simply by agreeing with His good opinion of us: "Father, You love me. You see no fault in me. I stand holy and righteous before You because of what Jesus did for me! I am one with You!" We live exulting and rejoicing in His great love! As we do, that's how we begin to reign in this life. As long as you focus on yourself and your failures, you are living in condemnation, and it brings death. But when you focus on Jesus and His gift of righteousness, you really start to live.

Day 1

Two Men Brought Two Different Results: Condemnation vs Righteousness

Romans 5:12-17: *12 Therefore, as sin came into the world through one man, and death as the result of sin, so death spread to all men, [no one being able to stop it or to escape its power] because all men sinned. AMP*

13 Yes, people sinned even before the law was given. But it was not counted as sin because there was not yet any law to break. NLT

14 Still, everyone died – from the time of Adam to the time of Moses – even those who did not disobey an explicit command of God as Adam did. Now Adam is a symbol, a representation of Christ, who was yet to come. 15 But there is a great difference between Adam's sin and God's gracious gift. For the sin of this one man, Adam, brought death to many. But even greater is God's wonderful grace and His gift of forgiveness to many through this other Man, Jesus Christ. 16 And the result of God's gracious gift is very different from the result of that one man's sin. For Adam's sin led to condemnation, but God's free gift leads to our being made right with God, even though we are guilty of many sins. 17 For the sin of this one man, Adam, caused death to rule over many. But even greater is God's wonderful grace and His gift of righteousness, for all who receive it will live in triumph over sin and death through this one Man, Jesus Christ. NLT

Romans 5:17: *For if because of one man's trespass (lapse, offense) death reigned through that one, much more surely will those who receive [God's] overflowing grace (unmerited favor) and the free gift of righteousness ... reign as kings in life through the one man Jesus Christ. AMP*

How did sin come into the world and what was its effect on man? (Verse 12)

At one time, we were all trapped in the power of sin. Condemnation, shame and guilt had dominion over us, and no one could escape sin's power because all men sinned.

What is the difference between Adam's sin and God's gracious gift? (verse 15)

What is the difference in the result of Adam's sin and God's gracious gift? (verse 16)

Who will escape sin's power and reign as a king in life through Jesus? (verse 17)

Adam's Sin: led to condemnation for all men

God's Gracious Gift: leads to man being made righteous through faith in Jesus

All men are trapped in condemnation and there's only one way to be set free: receive the gift of righteousness through Jesus! If believers who have been born-again, and have accepted Jesus as their Savior, do not understand the true Gospel — that they've been made righteous, acceptable, and approved, not based on their good works, but based on Jesus' finished work — they will live trapped in condemnation. Romans 5:17 teaches us that because of sin, condemnation was able to reign in every person's life, but those who receive the abundance of grace and the free gift of righteousness will triumph over sin and reign in life as kings through relying upon Jesus.

What does it mean to receive God's grace and his gift of righteousness?

The word *receive* (G2983 Strong's) means: "to take on, to get a hold of, to seize, to accept."

When you receive His gift of righteousness, you **take on** his identity. You **lay hold of** His good opinion of you. You **accept** the truth that what the Father says about you in Christ is true! That's how you reign in life through Jesus, by agreeing with the Father's good opinion of you in Christ.

Those who hold on to their own opinion, such as, "I'm not good enough. There's something wrong with me," will live in condemnation, and the power of sin will be able to reign in their lives. But those who receive the gift of righteousness by agreeing with their Father's opinion, such as, "I am approved, accepted, holy, blessed and favored in Jesus," will be able to live free from sin's power to condemn them, and will reign in life as kings!

Up until I was in my mid 20s, condemnation was able to reign in my life because I took on my own opinion of myself instead of God's. Thoughts like, "I'm not good enough;" "I lack in some way;" "I have to pay for my sins;" "They are better than me," and "They don't like me," were my opinion of myself. But my whole life changed when I became willing to lay down my own opinion and truly embrace my Father's good opinion of me in Jesus. When I did, sin lost it's power to condemn me as I embraced my new identity in Christ. That is what it means to triumph over sin and reign in life through Jesus!

What did you learn today about what it means to reign as a king in life through Jesus?

What Does It Mean to Reign in Life?

Romans 5:17

Take time to pray before you begin.

Today we will look at real life examples of what it looks like to reign in life through Jesus. Let's take a look at Romans 5:17 again:

> Romans 5:17: *For if because of one man's trespass (lapse, offense) death reigned through that one, much more surely will those who receive [God's] overflowing grace (unmerited favor) and the free gift of righteousness ... reign as kings in life through the one man Jesus Christ. AMP*

Who will reign in life through Jesus?

____

____

The Scriptures say that those who receive God's overflowing grace and His gift of righteousness will reign in life as kings through Jesus. But what does that look like in our everyday lives? How do we reign in life as kings when it comes to our health, finances, marriage, self-image, decisions, and the daily challenges we encounter?

Grace is the power of the Holy Spirit that enables us to believe who we are in Jesus, and trust Him with our lives. It is His unmerited favor and ability working in our hearts and our lives to bring God's promise to pass. When you receive His grace, you depend on His ability in you and not your own effort.

Righteousness is God's free gift to us of forgiveness and qualification. When you receive this gift of righteousness, you don't try to qualify yourself by anything you do, but you embrace the truth that you are blessed and qualified for every promise because of what Jesus did for you!

Let's take a look at how we make decisions when we are reigning in life as a king. Decision-making can cause lots of worry and anxiety when we depend on ourselves. Condemning, negative thoughts such as, "What if I make the wrong decision? I don't know what to do! What if I can't hear from God?" These kind of questions can cause fear to reign in our hearts.

Now, in each of these questions, who is the focus? Whose ability is being depended on?

____

Any time you depend on yourself, instead of receiving the grace (favor and ability) of God, condemnation will reign in your life. I used to depend on myself all the time and was always concerned about making the wrong decisions. Thank goodness, the Holy Spirit began to teach me how to receive His grace and embrace His gift of righteousness, and I began to live free from fear and reign through Jesus.

Reigning in Your Decisions

Several years ago my husband had to make a major decision regarding his business. He shared with me that he was thinking about letting go of a major source of our income in order to try something else. His decision could have potentially affected us in a very negative way. So I was presented with two choices: I could depend on my husband's ability to make the right decision and worry and fret about it, or I could receive God's grace and embrace His righteousness and live in peace. This was how I chose to respond, "Honey, you hear from God (John 10:5). You are led by His Spirit (Romans 8:14). God will direct you and cause your thoughts to be agreeable to His will (Proverbs 16:3). You'll make the right decision and God will work this out for our good."

I walked away from that conversation with my husband, and went away to a quiet spot to have a personal conversation with my Father God. I shared my heart with Him by saying, "Father, thank You for Your grace to trust You with this decision. Tell me once again what You say." In the quietness of my heart, I heard Him speak, "Connie, I live in Tony and he hears My voice. I am causing his thoughts to be agreeable to My will and his plans will be established and succeed." Peace filled my heart as I responded to His love for me, "Father, I trust You to lead and guide him. You will cause his thoughts to be agreeable to Your will. He is a success because of Jesus." I rested in the truth that it wasn't Tony's responsibility to hear from God, but rather God's promise to cause Tony's heart to be in agreement with His will. What peace this truth brought my heart!

Tony made the decision to let go of that major source of income, and I was able to enter into rest, knowing that it was all going to work out for our good. I was able to reign in life with peace in my heart as I continued to agree with what my Father had said. Every time I thought about the situation, I would talk to Him about what He had promised, and thanksgiving would rise up in my heart.

A couple of months later, this same company that Tony had decided to drop, approached him wanting to work with him again. Only this time, they were offering to increase his commission by one third! I realized that this had been God's plan all along to bring increase into our lives. If Tony had not let that company go, there would have been no need for them to offer him such a big increase to get him back. This situation showed me how worry and fear could have kept God's blessings from us. If I had depended on my own ability and logic, I would have convinced my husband to hold on to that source of income, and the power of God's grace (His ability) would not have been at work to bring this huge blessing into our lives. This experience further convinced my heart, that I reign in life — live free from condemnation and fear — and experience God's best for me when I receive

His grace and gift of righteousness by relying upon Jesus!

You reign in life by relying upon Jesus and coming into agreement with what you hear the Father speak to you about every situation in your life. It's about having an intimate, trusting relationship with the One who loves and cares for you the most.

In every situation of our lives we are given the choice between life or death. We can choose to depend on ourselves, or we can receive His grace by relying upon Jesus. We can try to qualify ourselves by our good works, or we can receive His gift of righteousness and rest in the truth that we are qualified for all of God's promises because of Jesus.

Reigning in Your Finances

Let's look at a financial example of what it means to reign in life through Jesus. When condemnation is reigning in your life, your mind is filled with these kinds of negative thoughts: "I lack. I don't have enough. What am I going to do to take care of myself? How is this bad economy going to affect me? How am I going to pay this bill?"

In each of these questions, who is the focus? Whose ability is being depended on?

____

Jesus made you righteous so that you could live free from a condemned mindset. But what does being declared righteous mean when you are facing a bad economy or you lose your job? When you are reigning in life, you look to your Father God, and say, "What do You say about me, Father?" When you ask Him, He always reminds you of who you are in Jesus. He says: (put your name on the lines below)

____________________, in the time of famine, you will prosper. (Psalm 37:17-19)

____________________, you're the head and not the tail. (Deuteronomy 28:1-13)

____________________, I'll supply all your needs according to My riches in glory in Christ Jesus. (Philippians 4:19)

____________________, all grace abounds toward you so that you have all sufficiency in all things and abound in every good work. (2 Corinthians 9:8)

This is what Your Father says about you. So how do you reign as a king in the area of your finances? You reign as a king by embracing what your Father says about you in Christ: "Father, I know You love me. You made me righteous. Your grace abounds towards me. I have all sufficiency in all things. I am abundantly blessed in Jesus!" When you rely upon Jesus, the power of grace and righteousness works in your life, and you reign in life through Him.

When you live with a condemned mindset, your heart is filled with shame about the poor financial decisions you've made, and your heart tells you: "I have to pay for this. I made this mess, I'm going to have to clean it up." But when you live reigning in life, you say, "Father, what do You say about me in Christ?" and you hear the Father say, "Jesus paid the penalty for your sin. You don't have to pay anymore." "You're justified. It's just as if you've done everything right! Rest in my love, and watch as I clean up your mess!" You reign in life over condemnation and shame and guilt, and experience His salvation when you embrace what the Father says about you in Jesus.

Reigning in Relationships

I want to share one more personal example of what it means to reign in life through Jesus. When my youngest daughter, Victoria, was in the 6th grade, she was experiencing some struggles with her relationships at school. Her heart was hurting and she felt like the kids didn't like her. Now, I knew that my Father says that the children of the righteous are surrounded by favor (Psalm 5:12) and that they are mighty and blessed upon this earth (Psalm 112:2), but my circumstances were saying something quite different. Before I understood what I am teaching you right now, my mindset would have been one of condemnation with thoughts like, "Why is this happening? What am I doing wrong? I must not be doing something right, Lord. You said Victoria would have favor but that's not what she is experiencing." My heart would have been filled with worry and anger about this situation. But here was another opportunity for me to make a choice between life or death. I could either depend on myself by trying to fix the problem in my own power; or I could receive God's grace (His ability) and embrace what He said about Victoria and reign in this situation by relying upon Jesus.

So I turned my heart toward Him and shared my concerns about Victoria's heart. I asked, "Father, what do You say about Victoria?" I heard Him speak again, comforting my heart with His love. He reminded me one more time that I was righteous in Jesus and that Victoria was favored and blessed upon this earth. I replied, "I trust You, Father, to work this situation out for her good. I don't care what I see. You qualified me in Jesus to receive Your promise concerning Victoria, and You say she is surrounded by favor. You say that she is mighty and blessed upon this earth. You say that she has great peace. I can't fix this problem, but You can, Father, and I rest in Your love." Once again I found myself reigning as a king, free from a condemned mindset, free from fear, as I received His grace and righteousness by relying upon Jesus.

When we receive the power of grace, and the gift of righteousness, we will reign in life as a king through Jesus Christ!

I watched in amazement as the grace of God began to work in my heart, in Victoria's heart, and then in the hearts of her classmates. His grace abounded so much that during 7th grade she experienced great favor, and God surrounded her with wonderful friends. She even had an opportunity to lead a 7th grade Bible study with the *Inside Story* and all the girls who participated, loved it! I stood back and watched as God manifested His promise in her life.

When we rely upon ourselves, condemnation rules in our hearts; but every time we rely upon Jesus, we reign in life as a king! We can live free from a condemned mindset and experience the power of His grace transforming our hearts and manifesting His promise in our lives. When we receive the power of grace, and the gift of righteousness, we will reign in life as a king through Jesus Christ!

What did you learn today about the practical application of reigning in life through Jesus? How will you apply this to your own life?

Grace Reigns Through Righteousness

Romans 5:18-21

Take time to pray before you begin.

Today we'll finish up Romans Chapter 5. You can live free from the vicious cycle of sin and condemnation and reign in life through Jesus, because God's grace abounds towards you!

> Romans 5:18-21: *18 Yes, Adam's one sin brings condemnation for everyone, but Christ's one act of righteousness brings a right relationship with God and new life for everyone. 19 Because one person disobeyed God, many became sinners. But because one other person obeyed God, many will be made righteous. 20 God's law was given so that all people could see how sinful they were. But as people sinned more and more, God's wonderful grace became more abundant. NLT*
>
> *20 But where sin increased and abounded, grace (God's unmerited favor) has surpassed it and increased the more and superabounded, 21 so that, [just] as sin has reigned in death, [so] grace (His unearned and undeserved favor) might reign also through righteousness . . . which issues in eternal life through Jesus Christ. AMP*

What did Adam's one sin bring to everyone? (verse 18)

____

What did Christ's one act of righteousness bring to everyone? (verse 18)

____

What happened because Adam disobeyed God? (verse 19)

____

What happened because Jesus' obeyed God? (verse 19)

____

Why was God's law given? (verse 20)

____

What happened when people sinned? What is more powerful, sin or God's grace? (verse 20)

____

What reigns when a person lives in condemnation? (verse 21)

____

What reigns when a person embraces the gift of righteousness? (verse 21)

____

Adam vs Jesus

Now let's look at each verse individually and discuss how this truth applies to our lives.

Verses 18 and 19 show the difference between being in Adam (our old nature) and being in Jesus (our new nature). Adam's one sin brought condemnation to everyone. Since everyone was condemned, sin reigned in their lives. The only way of escape is through Jesus, whose obedience brought the gift of righteousness to everyone. It was His obedience, not yours, that made it possible for you to be declared righteous.

Verse 20 reveals that the law was given to man to show him that he was a sinner, but it had no power to change his nature. No matter how hard man tried to be good, at the end of day he was still a sinner. The law only served to increase man's awareness of his sin and failure. That is why, when a person is taught that they are righteous or qualified for God's blessing through their obedience to the law, it only produces more condemnation and more sin (2 Corinthians 3:6). The law condemns and keeps man trapped in the vicious cycle of sin.

But as sin increased and kept man under it's control, God's grace superabounded toward man and brought with it freedom from sin's power. Even though sin reigned in men's lives through condemnation, now grace reigns in men's lives through the gift of righteousness.

The Greek word for *reign* in verse 21 can be also be translated as "king." Sin was able to rule like a king through condemnation, and brought death to everyone. As long as you were declared a sinner and accepted that identity, condemnation brought death and destruction to your life.

Sin and condemnation used to rule and reign in your life, but now God's grace superabounds toward you. Grace rules as a king through righteousness, and brings all who are in Christ into eternal life (approval, acceptance, joy, peace, love, abundance, security). The gift of righteousness defends us against all the accusations and lies of the devil.

When a person is guilt-ridden and condemned, sin's power is particularly devastating, negatively affecting every area of their life. But those who embrace the gift of righteousness by embracing their new identity in Jesus, will ultimately experience the glorious life Jesus has provided. Those who understand that righteousness is a gift to be received, and not a wage to be earned, are the ones who will reign like kings over sin and all its effects, in this life.

Now a king is one who is in authority, who decides and decrees a thing and it is established. Whatever the king or ruler decides is what ultimately happens in the lives of the people over which he reigns.

The power of sin reigns through condemnation, which is simply a negative opinion of yourself. Here are some examples of condemning, negative thoughts:

I'm not good enough

I can't do it

I'm ugly

I hate myself

I'm a failure

I am not worthy

When you embrace these lies as who you are, sin's power is able to rule over your life and produce guilt, shame, depression, discouragement, fear, worry, and insecurity in your heart.

On the other hand, the power of grace reigns through righteousness, which is simply embracing the Father's good opinion of you in Christ:

I am good in Jesus

I can do all things through Christ who strengthens me

I am beautiful in every way! There is no flaw in me

I love myself because Jesus proved that I am worthy of love

I am a success in Jesus!

*I am qualified **because of Jesus!***

When you embrace the truth of your new identity in Jesus, the power of grace rules in your life, and produces peace, joy, love, health, abundance, and security in your heart.

The person who believes that it is their good works that make them approved and favored by God, or that they have to do something to be qualified for God's blessing, will never reign in this life. It is only when you receive God's grace and His gift of righteousness, that you'll reign in every area of your life, through Jesus. No longer will the devil be able to accuse you. No longer will you live under the accusations that something is wrong with you, that you are not good enough, or that you don't qualify. Any trial that you face is a temptation or circumstance attempting to convince you that what God says about you isn't true. When you reign in life, it doesn't matter what you see. The only thing that matters is, "Father, what do You say about me?" As you continue to receive God's grace, you'll begin to speak in agreement with your Father's good opinion of you in Christ, and you'll find that what you decide and decree will be established in your life.

> Job 22:28: *You shall also decide and decree a thing and it shall be established for you; and the light [of God's favor] shall shine upon your ways. AMP*

According to this verse, what does it look like to reign in life as a king through Jesus?

____

____

Agree with the King

When you and I speak in agreement with the King of kings and we agree with His opinion of us in Christ, the light of God's favor shines upon our ways. We are kings of the King, we simply carry out the will of our Father by listening to Him speak to our hearts, and then declaring His opinion of us in Christ.

If the King says you are forgiven and approved, then that's what you say!

If the King says your children are mighty and blessed upon the earth, then that's what you say!

If the King says you are abundantly blessed, then that's what you say!

If the King says you are complete and you lack nothing, then that's what you say!

If the King says everything works together for your good, then that's what you say!

If you continue to hold on to your own opinion, condemnation will reign in your life. You'll experience sadness, disappointment, fear, discouragement, shame, condemnation and confusion. But if you will embrace your Father's good opinion of you in Christ, you'll see the power of God's grace reigning in your life. You will experience peace, joy, love, security, and victory in every area of your life. As you decide and decree what the King says, then what the King says is established in your life. That's what it means to reign in life as a king through Jesus!

Now let's finish today's study by reading Romans 5:16-21 in the Message Bible.

> *16 There's no comparison between that death-dealing sin and this generous, life-giving gift. The verdict on that one sin was the death sentence; the verdict on the many sins that followed was this wonderful life sentence. 17 If death got the upper hand through one man's wrongdoing, can you imagine the breathtaking recovery life makes, sovereign life, in those who grasp with both hands this wildly extravagant life-gift, this grand setting-everything-right, that the one man Jesus Christ provides? 18 Here it is in a nutshell: Just as one person did it wrong and got us in all this trouble with sin and death, another person did it right and got us out of it. But more than just getting us out of trouble, he got us into life! 19 One man said no to God and put many people in the wrong; one man said yes to God and put many in the right. 20 All that passing laws against sin did was produce more lawbreakers. But sin didn't, and doesn't, have a chance in competition with the aggressive forgiveness we call grace. When it's sin versus grace, grace wins hands down. 21 All sin can do is threaten us with death, and that's the end of it. Grace, because God is putting everything together again through the Messiah, invites us into life — a life that goes on and on and on, world without end.*

Day 3

So Awake to Righteousness!

If what Adam did brought all of us under the power of sin and condemnation, how much more did Jesus bring us all into the power of righteousness and life? If the power of sin reigns when we embrace a negative opinion of ourselves, how much more will the power of grace reign when we grasp with both hands the good opinion our Father has of us in Christ? When it is sin versus grace, grace wins every time! When you bring any negative opinion of yourself into the light of grace, condemnation loses its power to rule in your life. So bring your heart to Jesus. Embrace with both hands His extravagant gift of righteousness. Decide and decree what the King says and reign in life through Jesus!

What did you learn this week about what it means to reign in life as a king through Jesus? How will you apply this truth to your life?

Week 6

Dead to Sin; Alive in Christ

Romans Chapter 6

Day 1

Dead to Sin

Day 2

Sin Has Lost Its Power

Day 3

Say "Yes" to Jesus

This week we'll study Romans chapter Six. In the first five chapters of the book of Romans, the Apostle Paul shared the Good News about Jesus. He repeatedly emphasized that we've been made righteous and qualified for God's blessings, not through our good works, but through our reliance upon Jesus. When people hear that being approved by God has nothing to do with their obedience, the question often arises, "Does that mean that it is okay to live in sin?" This often causes pastors and teachers to be reluctant to share this wonderful Gospel of Grace out of concern that people will use it as a license to sin. This is a lie of the devil designed to keep God's children from living free from sin. We will address this lie in this week's study and clearly see that God's grace is greater than sin, and gives us the power to live a righteous life.

Dead to Sin

Romans 6:1-5

Take time to pray before you begin.

Today we will look at Romans 6:1-5:

> *1 Well then, should we keep on sinning so that God can show us more and more of His wonderful grace? 2 Of course not! Since we have died to sin, how can we continue to live in it? 3 Or have you forgotten that when we were joined with Christ Jesus in baptism, we joined Him in His death? NLT 4 We were buried therefore with Him by the baptism into death, so that just as Christ was raised from the dead by the glorious [power] of the Father, so we too might [habitually] live and behave in newness of life. 5 For if we have become one with Him by sharing a death like His, we shall also be [one with Him in sharing] His resurrection [by a new life lived for God]. AMP*

When the Good News of God's grace is preached, what question often arises in people's minds? (verse 1)

____

____

What is the answer to this question? (verse 2)

____

____

The Apostle Paul taught grace so radically that people began to question if it was okay to live in sin. In the first five chapters of Romans, Paul taught very clearly that it's not your obedience to the law that makes you righteous, but rather your faith in Jesus. He explained that if you are in Christ, your sins will never disqualify you and your good works will never qualify you. You are qualified for all of God's blessings because you have been made righteous through faith in Jesus. God is no longer holding your sins against you and He has completely cleared your record forever. God's grace is greater than all your sins! So it was only natural for the question to arise, "If I am righteous and blessed by God through my faith in Jesus, is it okay to continue to live in sin so God can continue to show me more grace?" In verse 2 the Apostle Paul answers emphatically, "Of course not!" Sin still puts people in bondage and destroys their lives. The very reason Jesus came was to free you from sin's power so that you could experience an abundant life. Grace is the power to live free from sin, not an excuse to live in bondage to it.

What Exactly is Sin?

In verse 2 the word *sin* comes from the Greek word, *hamartia.* It is a noun describing the sin nature. In several translations of the Bible, this word is often translated "the old self." In other words, Paul was saying, "Of course not! If your old sinful self died with Jesus, then how can you continue to live in sin? A sinner lives in sin, but you're not a sinner anymore! Sin is no longer a part of your nature. You've been given a brand new righteous nature in Jesus. Righteous people live righteous lives. You have a new DNA, which is LOVE, and you are made in the very image of your Father, Who is LOVE! We love because He first loved us and it is who we are in Jesus!

We have a new motivation for not living in sin. It's no longer because we fear punishment from God or we are trying to earn His approval. It's simply because we realize it no longer has any more power over us. It's not who we are! If Jesus set us free from sin's dominion and the destruction it brings, why would we want to become a slave to it once again? We now have the power to live a righteous, blessed life through Jesus. We can experience the glorious life we have always wanted to live.

In verse 3, what did the Apostle Paul ask if we've forgotten?

____

____

How was Jesus raised from the dead? How are we able to live and behave in newness of life? (verse 4)

____

____

If you were made one with Jesus in His death, what is also true of you? (verse 5)

____

____

____

The Apostle Paul continues in verse 3 by saying, "Have you forgotten that you've been made one with Jesus?" When Jesus died for your sin, your sin nature died with Him. When Jesus rose again, your new righteous nature rose up with Him. Verse 4 explains how the glorious power that raised Jesus from the dead is the very same power that lives in you and empowers you to live and behave in newness of life. As we depend on His power within us, sin loses its control in our lives.

> Philippians 2:13 says, *"[Not in your own strength], for it is God Who is all the while effectually at work in you [energizing and creating in you the power and desire], both to will and to work for His good pleasure...." AMP*

What does God's resurrection power create within us?

____

____

When we think of living in sin our minds often go to things like lying, greed, murder, adultery, stealing, fornication or drunkenness, but sin is also strife, jealousy, worry, fear, offense, unforgiveness, resentment, disrespect, gossip, or criticizing and judging people. Every one of these things brings destruction to our hearts and to our lives. That's why it is such Good News that Jesus set us free by changing the very core of our being and empowering us by His Spirit to live free from sin. None of these things describe who we are anymore. We have a new righteous nature in Jesus. Our new nature is loving, joyful, peaceful, good, kind, patient, faithful, humble, and self-controlled because Jesus lives in us! As we look to Jesus for strength, His resurrection power brings this good fruit out in our lives. (Galatians 5:22-23)

When we remember this, we experience the power that helps us overcome temptation. For example, let's put some of these words into the verses we studied today so we can practically apply this to our lives:

> Well then, should we keep on *worrying* so that God can show us more and more of his wonderful grace? Of course not! Since we have died to *worry*, how can we continue to live in it? Have you forgotten that just as your old fearful self died with Jesus, your new confident self rose up with Him. And the very same glorious power that raised Jesus from the dead now lives in you, and empowers you to live a new life of confidence and peace. As you rely upon Jesus, He lives His life through you.
>
> Well then, should we keep on *judging* people so that God can show us more and more of his wonderful grace? Of course not! Since we have died to *judgment*, how can we continue to live in it? Have you forgotten that just as your old *judgmental* self died with Jesus, your new loving, compassionate self rose up with Him. You are one with Jesus! And the very same glorious power that raised Jesus from the dead now lives in you, and empowers you to live a new life of love and compassion. As you rely upon Jesus, He lives His life through you.
>
> Now insert something you have been tempted by in these verses:
>
> Well then, should I keep on ____________________ so that God can show me more and more of his wonderful grace? Of course not! Since I have died to ____________________, how can I continue to live in it? Have I forgotten that just as my old ______________________ self died with Jesus, my new ____________________ self rose up with Him. And the very same glorious power that raised Jesus from the dead, now lives in me, and empowers me to behave in newness of life. As I rely upon Jesus, He lives His life through me.

Recently, I was dealing with some negative feelings in my heart toward someone in my life. In the past, I would justify the way I felt, and these feelings would create resentment and offence in my heart, but now I know that this is not who I am in Jesus. Jesus made a way for me to live free from these negative feelings and the destruction that sin can bring into my life. He gave me a brand new righteous nature filled with His love and gave me His power to behave in newness of life. So once again, I turned my heart toward Jesus and asked Him to help me overcome this temptation to be upset and offended. As I shared my negative feelings with Him and trusted Him to strengthen me by His grace, sin lost its power in my life. When I remembered who I am, and asked Jesus to help me, the same glorious power that raised Him from the dead empowered me to love. I was, once again, amazed at the love and compassion that flowed from my heart towards this person, and I realize that it's Jesus living His life through me. That is what's so amazing about grace — it really does set you free from the power of sin!

Your sinful self died with Jesus on the cross and your new righteous self rose up with Him! You are one with Him! When you remember who you are in Jesus, and depend on His resurrection power within you, God's grace brings forth the fruit of love, joy, peace, and kindness in your life. It's not an effort. It's not a struggle. It's simply the fruit of abiding in Jesus. It's Jesus living His glorious life through you!

What did you learn from today's study and how will you apply it in your life?

Day 2

Sin Has Lost Its Power

Romans 6:6-14

Take time to pray before you begin.

Today we will continue with the Apostle Paul's thoughts from our previous study. In Romans 6:6-14 we will see that the very reason Jesus died for us was to break sin's power over our lives.

> Romans 6:6-14: *6 We know that our old sinful selves were crucified with Christ so that sin might lose its power in our lives. We are no longer slaves to sin 7 For when we died with Christ, we were set free from the power of sin. 8 And since we died with Christ, we know we also live with Him. 9 We are sure of this because Christ was raised from the dead, and He will never die again. Death no longer has any power over Him. 10 When He died, He died once to break the power of sin. But now that He lives, He lives for the glory of God. NLT 11 Even so <u>consider yourselves also dead to sin and your relation to it broken, but alive to God [living in unbroken fellowship with Him] in Christ Jesus</u>. 12 Let not sin therefore rule as king in your mortal . . . bodies, to make you yield to its cravings and be subject to its lusts and evil passions. 13 Do not continue offering or yielding your bodily members to sin as instruments (tools) of wickedness. But offer and yield yourselves to God as though you had been raised from the dead to [perpetual] life, and your bodily members . . . to God, presenting them as implements of righteousness. 14 For sin shall not [any longer] exert dominion over you, since now you are not under Law [as slaves], but under grace [as subjects of God's favor and mercy]. AMP*

Why was your old sinful self crucified with Jesus? What are you no longer a slave to? (verse 6)

____

____

What happened when you died with Jesus? (verse 7)

____

____

Why did Jesus die? (verse 10)

____

What does the Apostle Paul tell you to consider about yourself? (verse 11)

____

____

What does verse 12 tell you not to yield to?

____

What does the Apostle Paul encourage you to yield yourself to in verse 13?

____

____

Why does sin no longer have any dominion over you? (verse 14)

____

____

We saw in a previous week that the power sin had over us was condemnation, guilt, and shame. The Bible says that the moment Adam and Eve sinned, shame entered their hearts. They immediately began feeling inferior and pulled away from their relationship with God. When we live sin-conscious, we continually live with a sense of not being good enough; lacking in some way; and finding fault with ourselves and others, just like Adam and Eve did. We are trapped in the vicious cycle of sin and condemnation just like the rest of the world (Romans 5:12).

But when Jesus died, our old sinful self died with Him. He died to break the power that sin had over our lives. By forgiving all our sins, and making us perfect, innocent, and righteous in our Father's sight, Jesus made a way for us to live free from condemnation. Instead of running from God when we fail, we now can run to Him, knowing His love and grace will heal our hearts and empower us to live righteous lives. Sin's power has been broken off of us because it no longer can keep us from an intimate, loving relationship with our Heavenly Father. He wants us to run to Him in our weakness and temptations so that He can reassure us of His love and remind us of our new nature, which is righteous, holy, and good because of Jesus!

Romans 6:10 says that Jesus died once to break the power sin had over us, but now He lives so that our lives might glorify God. But how do we live in the reality of this truth? The answer to this question is found in Romans 6:11.

Your Relationship with Sin Has Changed

> Romans 6:11: *"Even so consider yourselves dead to sin and your relation to it being broken, but alive to God [living in unbroken fellowship with Him] in Christ Jesus."* *AMP*

How do you practically experience freedom from the power of sin? You consider yourself dead to sin and your relationship to it broken. You no longer live sin-conscious, but live righteous-conscious by embracing your new identity in Jesus! Consider yourself righteous, approved, blessed, favored, qualified, forgiven and dearly loved by your Heavenly Father and live in unbroken fellowship with Him. You can talk to Him about the temptations you are facing, and ask Him for His grace to overcome because His good opinion of you never changes! When you consider yourself righteous in Jesus and live in unbroken fellowship with your Heavenly Father, righteous fruit will come out in your life!

Now let's look at verses 12-14 again:

> *12 Let not sin therefore rule as king in your mortal... bodies, to make you yield to its cravings and be subject to its lusts and evil passions.*
>
> *13 Do not continue offering or yielding your bodily members... to sin as instruments (tools) of wickedness. But offer and yield yourselves to God as though you have been raised from the dead to [perpetual] life, and your bodily members... to God, presenting them as implements of righteousness.*
>
> *14 For sin shall not [any longer] exert dominion over you, since now you are not under Law [as slaves], but under grace [as subjects of God's favor and mercy]. AMP*
>
> *14 Sin is no longer your master, for you no longer live under the requirements of the law. Instead, you live under the freedom of God's grace. NLT*

These verses reveal that even though Jesus set us free from the power of sin, we have a choice every day as to whether we are going to yield to sin's power and live in bondage or yield ourselves to God by considering ourselves dead to sin and alive in Christ. Sin loses its power in your life when you no longer live under the requirements of the law, but instead begin to live under the freedom of God's grace.

What does it truly mean to yield ourselves to God and His righteousness? What does it mean to live in the freedom of God's grace? In Galatians 2:19-21, the Apostle Paul shows us what it looks like to yield ourselves to God so we might truly live.

The Apostle Paul considered himself dead to sin and lived in unbroken fellowship with the One Who loved him

> Galatians 2:19-21: *19 For when I tried to keep the law, it condemned me. So I died to the law—I stopped trying to meet all its requirements—so that I might live for God. 20 My old self has been crucified with Christ. It is no longer I who live, but Christ lives in me. So I live in this earthly body by trusting in the Son of God, who loved me and gave Himself for me. 21 I do not treat the grace of God as meaningless. For if keeping the law could make us right with God, then there was no need for Christ to die. NLT*

What happened when the Apostle Paul tried to keep the law? (verse 19)

____

____

What did he do when trying to keep the law didn't work for him? (verse 19)

The Apostle Paul considered himself dead to sin. What did he say about himself in verse 20?

What truth did he explain in verse 21?

I can completely relate to Paul in these verses. I, too, tried my best to please God by trying to obey all His laws and commands, but it didn't work for me either. All the law had the power to do was condemn me and make me feel separated from God.

But God's grace completely set me free from the power of sin. I began to consider myself crucified with Jesus. When I realized my old sinful self was dead and that I was now one with Jesus, I began to truly live. My failures no longer made me feel unworthy, but rather caused me to run to the throne of grace, to receive His unconditional love and grace in my time of need (Hebrews 4:16). Like Paul, I began to live by trusting and relying upon Jesus and His great love for me. Now I no longer live under the requirements of the law, but I live in the freedom of God's grace, living in unbroken fellowship with Him. His grace empowers me to live free from the power of sin and its effects on my heart and life. Again, let's look at the difference between law and grace:

> **The Law** only showed us how sinful we were, and filled our hearts with condemnation, guilt and shame (Romans 5:20)
>
> **Grace** gives us the gift of Righteousness and empowers us to live a righteous life!

When you consider yourself dead to sin and alive in Jesus, you live in unbroken fellowship with Him, and sin loses it's power in your life. His grace empowers you to live a righteous life as you daily trust and rely upon Him!

What is the main truth that stood out to you today? How will you apply it to your life?

Say "Yes" to Jesus!

Romans 6:15-23

Take time to pray before you begin.

Today we will finish Romans chapter 6 and get a clear understanding that whoever you yield to (say yes to) controls your life. So choose to say "yes" to Jesus – identify yourself completely with Him!

> Romans 6:15-23: *15 What then [are we to conclude]? Shall we sin because we live not under the Law but under God's favor and mercy? Certainly not! 16 Do you not know that if you continually surrender yourselves to anyone to do his will, you are the slaves of him whom you obey, whether that be to sin, which leads to death, or to obedience, which leads to righteousness? 17 But thank God, though you were once slaves of sin, you have become obedient with all your heart to the standard of teaching in which you were instructed and to which you were committed. 18 And having been set free from sin, you have become the servants of righteousness. 19 I am speaking in familiar human terms because of your natural limitations. For as you yielded your bodily members as servants to impurity and ever increasing lawlessness, so now yield your bodily members once for all as servants to righteousness [which leads] to sanctification. 20 For when you were slaves to sin, you were freed in regard to righteousness. 21 But then what benefit (return) did you get from things of which you are now ashamed? 22 But now since you have been set free from sin and have become the slaves of God, you have your present reward in holiness and its end is eternal life. 23 For the wages which sin pays is death, but the [bountiful] free gift of God is eternal life through (in union with) Jesus Christ our Lord. AMP*

What question does the Apostle Paul ask again in verse 15?

____

____

____

Who is a person a slave to? (verse 16)

____

____

____

What instructions did the Apostle Paul give you in verse 19?

____

____

What are the wages which sin pays? (verse 23)

____

What is the free gift of God? (verse 23)

____

____

In Verse 16, the word *obey* comes from the Greek word *hupakouo* (G5219 Strong's) and it means: "to hear under (as a subordinate), that is, to listen attentively."

Whoever you listen attentively to is who you become enslaved to and who controls your life.

Listen attentively to sin (the devil) = Condemnation and death

Listen attentively to righteousness (Jesus) = Freedom

As a believer, the enemy wants to keep you enslaved to sin; so he tempts you to believe lies such as: "You can't trust God! God isn't going to come through for you. You need to fix this problem on your own. Nobody really cares about you. Everyone else is doing it so it must be okay." When you listen to these lies and agree with them, it produces the works of the flesh in your life (Galatians 5:17-21) and the result is condemnation and shame (Romans 6:21).

On the other hand, the Spirit of God lives within you and He empowers you to live free from sin. When you turn to Him, you'll hear Him say, "That's not who you are! You are loved, righteous, good, kind, loving, blessed and favored because of Jesus. God is good and trustworthy and He works everything together for your good!" When you listen to the truth and agree with it, it produces the fruit of the spirit in your life (Galatians 5:22-23) and the result is abundant life (Romans 6:23).

So, we can either yield to sin and "listen attentively" to sin tell us what to do and stay enslaved to it; or we can yield to righteousness and "listen attentively" to Jesus as He tells us who we are, and reign in life through Him. Whoever we listen to determines the fruit of our lives.

Titus 2:11-12 says, *"For the grace of God has appeared that offers salvation to all people. 12 It teaches us to say "No" to ungodliness and worldly passions, and to live self-controlled, upright and godly lives in this present age. NIV*

What does grace teach us to do?

Let's end this week by reading Romans 6:15-23 out of the Message Bible:

15-18 So, since we're out from under the old tyranny, does that mean we can live any old way we want? Since we're free in the freedom of God, can we do anything that comes to mind? Hardly. You know well enough from your own experience that there are some acts of so-called freedom that destroy freedom. Offer yourselves to sin, for instance, and it›s your last free act. But offer yourselves to the ways of God and the freedom never quits. All your lives you've let sin tell you what to do. But thank God you've started listening to a new master, one whose commands set you free to live openly in his freedom! 19 I'm using this freedom language because it's easy to picture. You can readily recall, can't you, how at one time the more you did just what you felt like doing—not caring about others, not caring about God—the worse your life became and the less freedom you had? And how much different is it now as you live in God's freedom, your lives healed and expansive in holiness? 20-21 As long as you did what you felt like doing, ignoring God, you didn't have to bother with right thinking or right living, or right anything for that matter. But do you call that a free life? What did you get out of it? Nothing you're proud of now. Where did it get you? A dead end. 22-23 But now that you've found you don't have to listen to sin tell you what to do, and have discovered the delight of listening to God telling you, what a surprise! A whole, healed, put-together life right now, with more and more of life on the way! Work hard for sin your whole life and your pension is death. But God's gift is real life, eternal life, delivered by Jesus, our Master.

What happens in your life when you say yes to sin? (verses 19-21)

What happens in your life when you say yes to Jesus? (verses 22-23)

Saying yes to sin leads you down a path of condemnation and death, but saying yes to Jesus leads you down a path to a whole, healed, put together life. God gives us the choice between life and death, and then gives us the grace to choose life so that we can live in the freedom that Jesus died for us to have. Sin is no longer your master! Sin has lost its power in your life, so say yes to Jesus and live free from sin and its effects on your heart and life.

So Awake to Righteousness and say "Yes" to Jesus!

I am dead to sin and alive in Christ! I am no longer a sinner. I am righteous in Jesus. My failures no longer separate me from my Heavenly Father. I live in unbroken fellowship with Him. I say no to sin, and I say yes to Jesus – I am approved, accepted, forgiven, blessed, loving, kind, forgiving, peaceful, and very good because of Jesus! Because of Jesus, sin has lost its power in my life and I am free to let Jesus live His life through me!

What is the main truth you learned today and how will you apply it in your life?

No Longer Schizophrenic

Romans 7

Day 1

You Have the Perfect Husband

Day 2

The Struggle of Being Married to the Law

Day 3

Living Free from a Condemned Mindset!

You Have the Perfect Husband

Romans 7:1-6

Take time to pray before you begin.

This week we will study Romans chapter 7. In this chapter of Romans, the Apostle Paul explains the condition of a person's mind who is confused about their new identity in Jesus. Schizophrenia is a condition of the mind in which a person is confused about who they are and has lost the sense of what is true. This causes them to be unstable in their emotions. When a child of God is still trying to gain approval and acceptance by God through their behavior, they live in a state of spiritual schizophrenia. They are confused about who they are and what is true about them. I remember when I used to be so confused about my true identity. I thought my behavior defined who I am, so when I did good, I considered myself good, but when I failed, I considered myself bad. Was I righteous or unrighteous? Was I qualified or unqualified? Had I done enough to please God or did I need to do more? I came to the conclusion that there was something wrong with me because I just could not get it right. This kept me in a constant state of confusion about my true identity which affected my emotions negatively. I did not experience the peace that was promised to me in Jesus.

When I realized that I was no longer bound to the law and its requirements of me, I was set free from spiritual schizophrenia. I realized that my identity did not come from my good or bad behavior, but rather through my union with Jesus. Jesus is my new husband. I have become one with Him. He gave me His identity and my failures can never change who I am on the inside. This has brought emotional stability and the peace that passes understanding to my heart and life. In today's study, you will learn how you, too, can live free from spiritual schizophrenia and live secure in your new identity in Jesus!

You are no longer bound to the law.

You have a new husband — His name is Jesus.

Romans 7:1-6: *1 Now, dear brothers and sisters — you who are familiar with the law — don't you know that the law applies only while a person is living? 2 For example, when a woman marries, the law binds her to her husband as long as he is alive. But if he dies, the laws of marriage no longer apply to her. 3 So while her husband is alive, she would be committing adultery if she married another man. But if her husband dies, she is free from that law and does not commit adultery when she remarries.*

4 So, my dear brothers and sisters, this is the point: You died to the power of the law when you died with Christ. And now you are united with the One who was raised from the dead. As a result, we can produce a harvest of good deeds for God. NLT 4 Therefore, my brethren, you also have become dead to the law through the body of Christ, that you may be married to another—to Him who was raised from the dead, that we should bear fruit to God. NKJV 5 When we were controlled by our old nature, sinful desires were at work within us, and the law aroused these evil desires that produced a harvest of sinful deeds, resulting in death [or condemnation] [Author's Insertion]. 6 But now we have been released from the law, for we died to it and are no longer captive to its power. Now we can serve God, not in the old way of obeying the letter of the law, but in the new way of living in the Spirit. NLT

Who does the law apply to? (verse 1)

____

When did you die to the power of the law? (verse 4)

____

Now who are you married to? And what is the result of this union? (verse 4)

____

When you were bound to the law, what did it produce in your life? (verse 5)

____

____

Now that you have been released from the law, how is your new life different? (verse 6)

____

____

In verses 1-3, the Apostle Paul addressed those who were familiar with Old Testament law. In the Old Testament, the law gave the wife no option of divorce. The man could divorce his wife (Deuteronomy 24:1), but the wife could not divorce her husband. Therefore, the only hope a woman could have of being freed from a man that didn't treat her right was for one of them to die. The Apostle Paul used this illustration to show us that we were once married to the law. The law defined who we were. It showed us our sin and condemned us and made us feel like we could never be good enough. He explained that the only way we could ever be free from this union with the law that enslaved us to sin was if a death occurred.

The Good News is a death has occurred! When Jesus died on the cross, your old sinful self died with Him and you were released from the requirements of the law. You were free to marry another. When you said, "Yes!" to Jesus, you rose again in union with Him. He gave you His very identity as His bride. You are now married to Jesus, Who was raised from the dead to make you one with Him. When you were joined with Him, He became your new husband.

Now look again at verses 5 and 6. Here the Apostle Paul explained that when we were married to the law, sinful desires produced sinful deeds which resulted in condemnation in our hearts. The only power the law had was to show us how we didn't measure up (Romans 3:20). But now that we are no longer captive to it's power, it can no longer judge us guilty, so now we can enjoy our relationship with our new husband, Jesus! In contrast to the law, we don't have to try to keep our new husband happy by trying to live up to his standards, rather we live by responding to His unconditional love for us. We love Him because He first loved us (1 John 4:19). He tells us that we are perfect in His sight and as we receive His love, the Spirit of grace empowers us to live a righteous life. (Galatians 5:22-23). Romans 7:6 shows us that we are now free to honor our new husband Jesus, not by the old way of trying to obey the letter of the law, but in the new way of living in the Spirit.

Being Married to the Law vs Being Married to Jesus

The law is like being married to a perfectionist — no matter what you do, you'll never be good enough; you'll never be approved. Being married to Jesus is like being married to the perfect husband — He sees only perfection in you! He never brings up your mistakes or holds your past against you. You are completely approved and unconditionally loved by Him.

The contrast between being married to the law and being married to Jesus is amazing. While the law says, "serve me," Jesus says, "I came to serve you." While the law demands, "Wash my feet," Jesus says, "Let me wash yours." The law says, "Try harder!" Jesus says, "Let me do it for you!" The law says "There's one more thing you need to do." Jesus says, "You're perfected forever, I see no flaw in you!" While the law condemns by saying, "You'll never be good enough," Jesus cleanses your heart from all shame by saying, "My beloved, you are very good, now rest in My love for you." See, so many Christians still see themselves married to the law and that's why they live in a constant struggle of condemnation and sin, but thank goodness, you now understand that you've died to the law and your new husband is Jesus!

> Isaiah 54:4-5 says, *4 "Fear not; you will no longer live in shame. Don't be afraid; there is no more disgrace for you… 5 For your Creator will be your husband; the LORD of Heaven's Armies is his name! He is your Redeemer, the Holy One of Israel, the God of all the earth.*

When you understand that you're no longer under the requirements of the law, and that your new husband is Jesus, what will you live free from? (verse 4)

You'll no longer live in fear or shame when you realize you're no longer bound to the law, but instead you're married to Jesus. Your heart will rejoice when you realize He has clothed you with dignity and honor as His beloved bride.

Isaiah 61:10 says, *"I am overwhelmed with joy in the LORD my God! For he has dressed me with the clothing of salvation and draped me in a robe of righteousness. I am like a bridegroom in his wedding suit or a bride with her jewels." NLT*

When you are married to someone you take on their identity — you become one with them. Everything they have now belongs to you. When I was born my name was Connie Beckham. Then one day Tony Witter came along and chose me and asked me to be his bride. When I said, "Yes," to him, my identity changed, and my new name became Connie Witter. We are now one — everything he has belongs to me and everything I have belongs to him.

The same is true with your relationship with Jesus. The Bible says that even when you were a sinner, Jesus loved you and died for you. He chose you and asked you to be his bride. When you said, "Yes!" to Him, your identity changed, your new name became Mrs. I AM! You became one with Him — everything He has belongs to you and everything you have belongs to Him! When I said "Yes" to Jesus, I became Mrs. I AM: righteous, holy, innocent, blessed, qualified, favored, and approved because I AM married to Jesus! You and I can rest in His abundant provision for us because we are His beloved bride!

Ephesians 5:25-27: *25 For husbands, this means love your wives, just as Christ loved the church. He gave up His life for her 26 to make her holy and clean, washed by the cleansing of God's word. 27 He did this to present her to himself as a glorious church without a spot or wrinkle or any other blemish. Instead, she will be holy and without fault.*

Why did Jesus give his life for you?

____

How does He present you to Himself?

____

Ephesians 5:27 says that Jesus presents you to Himself holy and without a single fault. In Jude 1:24 it tells us again that Jesus presents you as His bride *"unblemished (blameless and faultless) before the presence of His glory in triumphant joy and exultation [with unspeakable, ecstatic delight]"*.

Listen to His words of love to you from Song of Solomon 4:7-9:

7 My darling, everything about you is beautiful, and there is nothing at all wrong with you. NCV

"7 You're beautiful from head to toe, my dear love, beautiful beyond compare, absolutely flawless. 8 Come with me... my bride. 9 You've captured my heart...You looked at me, and I fell in love. One look my way and I was hopelessly in love!" MSG

How does your heart feel when you hear Him speak these words of love to you?

____

Day 1

This is how your new husband, Jesus, feels about you, and how He cleanses you by washing you with His word. When you fail, he does not shame you or make you feel guilty for your mistakes. Instead, He cleanses your heart from all fear and shame by reminding you of who you are — He says, "My beloved, you are mine; you are perfect in every way; I see no flaw in you!" As you receive His love by agreeing with His good opinion of you, you live free from fear and shame and are changed from the inside out into His very image. You begin to look just like your new husband, Jesus, not by any effort of your own, but by His Spirit at work in you!

What is the main truth you learned today and how will you apply it in your life?

Day 2

The Struggle of Being Married to the Law

Romans 7:7-24

Take time to pray before you begin.

Today we'll continue our study on Romans Chapter 7. In verses 1-6, the Apostle Paul compared the difference between being married to the law with being married to Jesus. In verse 5 he explained what it is like to be married to the law, *"When we were controlled by our old nature, sinful desires were at work within us, and the law aroused these evil desires that produced a harvest of sinful deeds, resulting in death (or condemnation)." [Author's Inserts]* Then in verses 7-23, He goes on to give a clear description of the mindset of one who still sees themselves bound to the law:

> Romans 7:7-13: *7 Well then, am I suggesting that the law of God is sinful? Of course not! In fact, it was the law that showed me my sin. I would never have known that coveting is wrong if the law had not said, "You must not covet." 8 But sin used this command to arouse all kinds of covetous desires within me! If there were no law, sin would not have that power. 9 At one time I lived without understanding the law. But when I learned the command not to covet, for instance, the power of sin came to life, 10 and I died. So I discovered that the law's commands, which were supposed to bring life, brought spiritual death instead. 11 Sin took advantage of those commands and deceived me; it used the commands to kill me. 12 But still, the law itself is holy, and its commands are holy and right and good. 13 But how can that be? Did the law, which is good, cause my death? Of course not! Sin used what was good to bring about my condemnation to death. So we can see how terrible sin really is. It uses God's good commands for its own evil purposes. NLT*

In verse 7, what did the Apostle Paul say the law showed us?

____

What happened when we learned the commands of God? (verse 9)

____

God's commands were supposed to bring life, but what did the Apostle Paul say actually happened? (verse 10)

____

What is true about the law of God? (verse 12)

____

____

What caused death or condemnation in us? (verse 13)

____

In this passage of scripture, the Apostle Paul is showing us the power of sin. The law simply showed us what sin is. He gave us the example of jealousy. The law tells us not to be jealous of anyone, but it doesn't give us the power not to be jealous. So when we hear that command and we realize that we have been jealous, the law condemns us by judging us guilty of sin.

The law is righteous, holy and good, but if you look at the law outside of Jesus, it just serves to show you how unholy and unrighteous you are in contrast to it. It shows us what it looks like to be righteous, but gives us absolutely no power to be righteous. When the law is read to us it becomes obvious that we are not obeying it perfectly, and so the power of sin condemns us. Paul is emphasizing here that if a person continues to live under the requirements of the law in order to be righteous, they will never live free from the power of sin. The law will always condemn them and convince them that they are a slave of sin even though Jesus set them free.

Living under the law makes you feel Schizophrenic

> Romans 7:14-24: *14 So the trouble is not with the law, for it is spiritual and good. The trouble is with me, for I am all too human, a slave to sin. 15 I don't really understand myself, for I want to do what is right, but I don't do it. Instead, I do what I hate. 16 But if I know that what I am doing is wrong, this shows that I agree that the law is good. 17 So I am not the one doing wrong; it is sin living in me that does it. 18 And I know that nothing good lives in me, that is, in my sinful nature. I want to do what is right, but I can't. 19 I want to do what is good, but I don't. I don't want to do what is wrong, but I do it anyway. 20 But if I do what I don't want to do, I am not really the one doing wrong; it is sin living in me that does it. 21 I have discovered this principle of life—that when I want to do what is right, I inevitably do what is wrong. 22 I love God's law with all my heart. 23 But there is another power within me that is at <u>war with my mind</u>. This power makes me a slave to the sin that is still within me. 24 Oh, what a miserable person I am! Who will free me from this life that is dominated by sin and death? NLT*

In Romans 7:14-24, the Apostle Paul describes the constant struggle with sin that goes on within the soul of a man who still sees himself married to the law.

Have you ever felt the way he describes?

Where is the war going on within them? (verse 23)

How does a person feel who doesn't understand that they have been freed from the power of sin? (verse 24)

Day 2

This passage of scripture can be confusing if you don't understand that Paul is describing the mindset of a person who is still in bondage to the requirements of the law. They are still struggling to be made righteous by trying to obey it. It describes the way a person thinks who has not realized that sin has lost its power in their life. There is a war going on in their mind that tells them they are still a slave of sin.

If not understood in context, this passage of Scripture could give the wrong impression that it is natural for a Christian to be constantly struggling with two conflicting desires, (1) to sin, and (2) to obey God's law. In Romans 6:6 the Apostle Paul tells us we are no longer slaves of sin, but in Romans 7:14 he says the trouble is he is a slave of sin. Without clear understanding this breeds confusion and can make you feel schizophrenic. Have you ever read this passage and thought, "Huh? I must have two different natures: A righteous one, and a sinful one." Or "I have a good part of me, but then I have a bad part of me." What causes us to think this way is how we feel when we experience success or failure. When we fail, we think we are bad, but when we succeed, we think we are good. We think we are qualified when we do things right, and disqualified when we don't. It's like we have two different personalities and we aren't sure which one we truly are. In the natural, doctors would call that being schizophrenic. It's not how God wants us to live! Jesus came to set us free from a schizophrenic mindset.

I can remember many years ago reading this passage of Scripture and relating to the struggle that the Apostle Paul was describing. I wanted so badly to be good and pleasing to God, but I was constantly doing the thing I didn't want to do. I agreed that God's law was righteous, good, and holy, but I thought I must not be because I couldn't seem to measure up to its requirements. I had a righteous nature in me, but because my mind was not renewed to the truth that I was no longer a slave of sin, I was constantly finding myself failing and feeling condemned because I just couldn't get it right. Even though I had accepted Jesus as my Savior, I eventually found myself miserable and like the Apostle Paul describes, saying, *"Who will deliver me from this life that is dominated by sin and condemnation?"* I found the answer by embracing my new identity in Jesus. I began renewing my mind to the truth that I am no longer married to the law, and stopped trying to be made righteous through its requirements. I was no longer a slave of sin. Sin had lost its power to condemn me because Jesus made me righteous and I realized that I am married to Him! I no longer live with this schizophrenic mindset. The struggle in my mind with sin is now gone because

I embraced the truth that even though I fail, it does not change my identity! I am the beloved bride of the King of kings and He is hopelessly in love with me!

It's in embracing our new identity in Christ that we break free from this schizophrenic mindset and this struggle with sin. Jesus has already determined our value by choosing us as His bride. He proved His love for us by giving us His righteous nature, not based on our obedience to the law, but based on our saying, "Yes," to Him. Now we get to decide whether or not we are going to receive our new husband's love by taking on His name and agreeing with His loving, unchanging, good opinion of us. Am I qualified, or am I disqualified? Am I good, or am I bad? Am I a sinner, or am I righteous? As long as the answers to these questions are based on what you do right or wrong, you will remain in the schizophrenic mindset never really sure of who you are. But when the answers to these questions are based on what Jesus has done for you, you will break free to live a life free from fear and shame because you have embraced your new identity in Christ. And nothing you do right or wrong will ever change that! You are married to the King of kings! You are royalty! And when you renew your mind to that truth, you will begin to live the free life He came to give you!

> Jesus has already determined our value by choosing us as His bride. He has proved His love for us by giving us His righteous nature, not based on our obedience to the law, but based on our saying, "Yes," to Him.

So don't go back to that husband who is a perfectionist and makes you feel like you'll never be good enough, living enslaved to the law, when Jesus has paid the price to set you free! Wake up and remember who you are! You are qualified, righteous, holy, perfect, blessed, and favored because you are married to the perfect husband, Jesus! You are never disqualified. You are never a failure. You are never disapproved. You are never rejected. You are no longer a failure who is confused, fearful, disgraced, and rejected. That person died on the cross 2000 years ago, and a brand new person rose up in Christ Jesus. You are led by God's Spirit, blessed, confident, justified, innocent and accepted because of Jesus! Jesus has spoken life over you by reminding you that this is what is true about you! The fruit of your life — whether you live a miserable, enslaved life or you live a joyful, free life — is determined by whether or not you agree with Him! So embrace your new identity and receive Jesus' unconditional love for you. Enjoy the benefits of being married to the King of kings!

What is the main truth you learned today and how will you apply it in your life?

Living Free From a Condemned Mindset!

Romans 7:21-25; 8:1-2

Take time to pray before you begin.

Today we'll finish our study on Romans chapter 7. We learned yesterday that when a person believes that their identity is based on their performance it leads to a schizophrenic mindset. They become confused about who they truly are on the inside because they are still living under the power of sin, which is condemnation. Eventually this leads to feeling sad and discouraged and asking the question found in Romans 7:24. Let's read the verses that lead up to this question and discover the answer to freedom that is found in Romans 8:1-2:

> Romans 7:21-25: *21 I have discovered this principle of life—that when I want to do what is right, I inevitably do what is wrong. 22 I love God's law with all my heart. 23 But there is another power within me <u>that is at war with my mind</u>. This power makes me a slave to the sin that is still within me. 24 Oh, what a miserable person I am! <u>Who will free me from this life that is dominated by sin and death?</u> 25 Thank God! <u>The answer is in Jesus Christ our Lord</u>. So you see how it is: <u>In my mind</u> I really want to obey God's law, but because of my sinful nature I am a slave to sin. NLT*
> *25 I thank God—through Jesus Christ our Lord! So then, <u>with the mind</u> I myself serve the law of God, but <u>with the flesh</u> the law of sin. NKJV*

> Romans 8:1-2: *So now there is no condemnation for those who belong to Christ Jesus. 2 And because you belong to him, the power of the life-giving Spirit has freed you from the power of sin that leads to death. NLT*

When a person depends on their own power and ability what does it make them a slave to? (verse 23)

____

What is the fruit of a person's life who loves God's law, but is still trying to live up to it by depending on their own power? What question arises in their heart? (verse 24)

____

What is the answer to this question? Where will a person find freedom from a life dominated by sin and condemnation? (verse 25)

____

Day 3

What is true of you because you belong to Jesus? What has the spirit of life in Christ Jesus set you free from? (Romans 8:1-2)

Depending on your own ability leads to condemnation

Verses 21-24 describe the mindset of a person who is relying upon themselves and their own power to do things right. Life is hard and everything seems like a struggle. They want to do God's will, but depending on their own power leads them to feeling like a failure.

The law is simply a list of requirements we feel we have to do in order to feel good about ourselves. It's always based on our performance and our ability to do something well. But as we can see in these verses, this kind of thinking eventually leads us to the end of our own strength, and to the question in verse 24, "Who will free me from this feeling of condemnation, this condescending voice in my head, that tells me I'm just not good enough and I just can't get it right?"

In Romans 7:14-24, the Apostle Paul gave us a clear description of how a person thinks who is struggling with a condemned mindset.

> Verse 14: *The trouble is with me. I'm the problem. There is something wrong with me. I am a slave of sin!*
>
> Verse 15: *I don't understand myself! Who am I and why do I act the way I do?*
>
> Verse 15: *I want to do right, but I don't!*
>
> Verse 18: *Nothing good lives in me!*
>
> Verse 18: *I want to do right, but I can't!*
>
> Verse 24: *Will I ever be free from the power of sin that creates emotional instability in me?*

Have you ever struggled with these thoughts? How did they make you feel?

This condemned mindset is caused by defining yourself by your performance and ability instead of letting your union with Jesus define you. Let's look at Romans 7:25 again in both the New Living Translation and the New King James Versions of the Bible.

> Romans 7:25: *Thank God! <u>The answer is in Jesus Christ our Lord</u>. So you see how it is: <u>In my mind</u> I really want to obey God's law, but because of my <u>sinful nature</u> I am a slave to sin. NLT*
>
> Romans 7:25: *I thank God—through Jesus Christ our Lord! So then, <u>with the mind</u> I myself serve the law of God, but <u>with the flesh</u> the law of sin. NKJV*

In verse 25 the word "sinful nature" in the New Living Translation is translated "flesh" in the New King James version.

This word "flesh" actually refers to our human strength or ability. With this in mind, let's read this verse again to get a clearer understanding of the truth the Apostle Paul is teaching us: "The answer to living a life free from the power of sin and condemnation is to rely upon Jesus, and not myself. The problem is this: in my mind, I really want to obey God's law, but when I rely upon my own strength to do it, I become a slave to sin."

Depending on Jesus leads to life and peace

Thank God, the answer to the question in Romans 7:24, "Who will free me from this life dominated by sin and condemnation?" is found in Romans 7:25, "The answer is found in Jesus Christ my Lord!"

In Romans chapter 8, the Apostle Paul continued to explain what he meant when he said, **"The answer is in Jesus Christ our Lord."** Verse 1 says that there is no condemnation for those who belong to Jesus! When Jesus became your husband, not only did your identity change from a sinner to His righteous, royal bride, but you also received His ability to live a righteous life. The power of the life-giving spirit came to live inside of you and your "I can't do it in my own strength" attitude was changed to "but I can do all things through Christ who gives me strength!" (Philippians 4:13) You exchanged your weakness for His strength! Now not only can you live a life that is free from any condemnation associated with your weakness and failures, but you can also rely upon your husband, Jesus, to strengthen you by His Spirit to believe who you are in Him!

I shared in yesterday's study that I used to relate to what the Apostle Paul described in Romans chapter 7. I lived with a condemned mindset because I believed something was wrong with me and for some reason I just couldn't get it right. My identity was based on my performance so naturally I had a schizophrenic mindset, feeling good about myself when I did something well, and feeling bad about myself when I failed. I was confused about who I was, why I was here, and if my life had any purpose at all. This way of thinking caused me to constantly depend on myself and my own strength to be good enough and led to a sad and discouraged life. Even though I was married to Jesus, I lived like I was married to the law because I was constantly depending on myself instead of Him. But thank God, I don't live that way anymore! I began to understand who I am in Jesus and that the law had no more power to condemn me. Now, instead of my mind being consumed with my performance and my ability, my mind is being renewed daily to the truth that I am one with Jesus and His power and ability is at work in me! I no longer think or feel like the person described in Romans chapter 7 because I have found true freedom in embracing my new identity in Jesus! Just as the spirit of life in Christ Jesus has set me free from the law of sin and death, you too can live free in Jesus!

Because of Jesus, you and I are now free to live a new life, married to a new husband in the Spirit. There is no condemnation, no longer a battle in our minds concerning our identity, because we belong to Jesus! So, reject condemnation when it comes at you. When you hear those voices in your head, saying, "You're not good enough; you're never going to get it right, you can't do it, you're not really that valuable," turn your eyes upon Jesus and ask Him to strengthen you. Renew your mind to the truth that you are no longer married to the law, you belong to Jesus! Depend upon His strength to believe who you are in Him! When you rely upon Jesus, it leads to life and peace. You live free from condemnation and sin loses its power in your life! The struggle with sin is over! You have found the answer in Jesus!

So, awake to righteousness and reign as the royal bride of Christ you were meant to be! Renew your mind to the Truth and declare what is true about you; "I am no longer married to the law! I have a new husband, and His name is Jesus! I am perfect in His sight and there is absolutely nothing wrong with me! I am no longer schizophrenic, thinking that I am bad when I fail, and good when I accomplish something. My identity is found in Jesus and my strength to believe it comes from Him! The Spirit of life in Christ Jesus has set me free from a condemned mindset. I now have the mind of Christ! Jesus has set me free! I think just like Him!

How can you live free from a condemned mindset?

____

What is the main truth you learned today and how will you apply it in your life?

____

____

____

____

____

____

____

____

____

Week 8

You are Led by God's Spirit

Romans 8:1-14

Day 1

Living Free from Condemnation

Day 2

The Mind of the Flesh vs The Mind of the Spirit

Day 3

You Live in the Spirit

Day 1

Living Free from Condemnation

Romans 8:1-2

Take time to pray before you begin.

Today we'll take a closer look at Romans 8:1-2 in the Amplified Bible, and get an even deeper understanding of what the Apostle Paul meant when he wrote, **"there is no condemnation to those who are in Christ Jesus."** In the previous lesson, we learned that Romans 7:14-24 gave us a very clear picture of how a person with a condemned mindset thinks. Their mind is filled with thoughts like this, "I want to do right, but I keep failing. There's nothing good in me. I just can't seem to get it right. I can't do it. It's too hard. What a miserable person I am." Paul asked the question we all wanted to know, "Who will deliver me from this miserable person that I am?" And then he gave us the only answer to freedom: "Thank God, the answer is in Jesus Christ, our Lord."

The mind that is focused on Jesus lives free from condemnation.

> Romans 8:1-2: *THEREFORE, [there is] now no condemnation (no adjudging guilty of wrong) for those who are in Christ Jesus, who live [and] walk not after the dictates of the flesh, but after the dictates of the Spirit. 2 For the law of the Spirit of life [which is] in Christ Jesus [the law of our new being] has freed me from the law of sin and death. AMP*

How does the Amplified Bible define "no condemnation?" (verse 1)

___

Who will live free from condemnation? (verse 1)

___

What has the Spirit of life in Christ Jesus freed us from? (verse 2)

___

In Romans 7:7-25, the Apostle Paul revealed the truth of the impossibility of living a righteous life by depending on your own ability. He gave us a picture of what a person's life is like when their mind is focused on their inability to live up to the law's demands, living in a constant state of condemnation. But our Father God is so merciful. Inspired by the Spirit, the Apostle Paul goes on to reveal in Romans 8 how a person can live free from a condemned mindset.

In verse 1, the phrase, "**who live and <u>walk not</u> after the dictates of the flesh, but after the dictates of the Spirit,**" is not included in every version of the Bible. It was included by some of the translators to clarify what the Apostle Paul was teaching. He is contrasting the difference between the life of a person who has their mind on the flesh (Romans 7:14-25) and the life of a person who has their mind on the Spirit (Romans 8:1-3).

To really be able to apply what is being taught in these verses, we need to understand the difference between the flesh, and the Spirit:

> *Flesh:* man's ability: self-reliance, self-righteousness
>
> *Spirit:* God's ability in man; reliance upon Jesus; the gift of righteousness in Jesus

The word *walk* in this verse comes from the Greek Word G4043 *peripateo,* from G4012 and G3961; Strong's defines it as: "to tread all around, that is, walk at large (especially as proof of ability); to follow (as a companion): - be occupied with."

What is important for us to understand is that the word "walk" in verse 1 means to be "occupied with one's ability." So the true meaning of this verse is that there is no condemnation in the heart of the person who is not occupied with their own ability, but is occupied with the Spirit's ability in them.

For several years of my adult life I lived with a condemned mindset even though I was in Christ. This condemnation didn't come from the Father. It came from my own wrong thinking that I wasn't good enough, and my dependence on my own ability to do things right. During that time I would often hear that there was "no condemnation" for me because I was in Christ, but I never understood how to live free from it. I still felt condemned. What did it mean that I could live free from condemnation?

One of the very first things the Holy Spirit taught me was to take my mind off of myself and turn it toward Jesus; to stop relying upon my own strength and begin to look to His strength within me. The answer to living free from a condemned mindset was for my mind to be occupied with Jesus and not myself. You see, it's not about our ability or our good works; it's about His ability and His good work in us. When we become occupied with who we are in Christ, that's when we live free from condemnation. I've lived in condemnation and it kills: it kills your self image, your emotions, your relationships, your body, your dreams, and eventually your life. All condemnation does is produce death. Jesus came to set us free from a condemned mindset.

So, how do we live free from condemnation? By having our minds occupied with Jesus – who we are in Him! Let's look at verse 1 again, *"[there is] now no condemnation...for those who are <u>in Christ Jesus</u>, who walk not after <u>the dictates</u> of the flesh, but after <u>the dictates</u> of the Spirit."*

The word *dictate* means to speak as one who has authority. So our flesh speaks to us and the Spirit speaks to us, but who we are occupied with determines whether we experience freedom from a condemned mindset. The question is whose authority are we going to submit to? We decide who we are going to listen to and agree with. We decide who we are going to let control our lives — the voice of condemnation or the voice of righteousness!

The Spirit empowers us and reveals Jesus to our hearts, and says, "You are righteous in Jesus," "You are favored in Jesus," "You are qualified, accepted and approved in Jesus." The same Spirit that raised Jesus from the dead lives inside of us and He came to remind us of who we are in Jesus and to empower us to believe it! He's our Comforter, our Strengthener, and our Helper. When we turn our thoughts from our own ability and begin to occupy our mind with His ability in us, condemnation loses its power in our lives.

Allow me to share a personal experience. Just the other day, I was feeling tired and irritable and I was grouchy with my husband. I recognized these negative feelings in me so I turned my thoughts to Jesus and said, "Jesus, I am struggling here. I don't know why I am feeling this way. Help me." He showed me once again that during my day I had been relying upon myself and my own ability which caused me to feel frustrated, and my mind had been occupied with the voice of condemnation telling me, "It's too hard, I can't do it!" That is what caused me to feel tired and grumpy. I needed to be refreshed in His strength and love for me. So I took some time just to sit and talk with Jesus and ask Him to strengthen me. As my mind became occupied with Jesus and who I am in Him, I felt His Spirit bring peace to my heart. The Spirit of life in Christ Jesus set me free from sin and condemnation.

You don't have to settle for a life lived in condemnation because the law of the Spirit of life in Christ Jesus has set you free. The *law of the Spirit of life,* spoken of in Romans 8:2 means "the animating principle by which the Holy Spirit acts as the imparter of life." *[Vines New Testament]*

Jesus Himself was tempted in every way that we are. In the garden of Gethsemane He experienced fear, disappointment and even frustration with His friends, but He walked in the Spirit by turning His thoughts to His Father and receiving the power He needed to overcome.

Condemnation is caused by relying upon your own ability and occupying your mind with negative thoughts about yourself or your circumstances. This produces negative emotions. For instance, if you are feeling fear, discouragement, or depression, these are all symptoms of focusing on yourself, and occupying your mind with the voice of condemnation. If you do find yourself experiencing a negative mindset, don't be condemned by it. Just recognize your need for Jesus, and turn your thoughts to Him. There is no one in this world who is immune to negative thoughts. Jesus Himself was tempted in every way that we are. In the garden of Gethsemane He experienced fear, disappointment and even frustration with His friends, but He walked in the Spirit by turning His thoughts to His Father and receiving the power He needed to overcome. You, too, can walk in the Spirit by turning your thoughts to Jesus when these negative feelings emerge. As you depend on His strength within you, you'll find yourself thinking differently and living free from condemnation.

The life that the Holy Spirit imparts to you is your new identity in Christ. He empowers you by reminding you of who you are in Jesus. He says, "You are righteous, forgiven, accepted, blessed, qualified, successful, victorious, healed, and complete in Christ, and He also gives you the power to believe it! There is no condemnation for those who are in Christ Jesus, who are occupied not with their own ability and failures, but who live occupied with His ability in them. So turn your focus from yourself and your ability and keep your mind occupied with Jesus. You'll find yourself living free from condemnation, and enjoying the life that Jesus came to give you!

What is the main truth you learned in this lesson and how will you apply it to your life?

Day 2

The Mind of the Flesh vs The Mind of the Spirit

Roman 8:3-6

Take time to pray before you begin.

Today we will continue our study of Romans chapter 8. We'll begin in verse 3 and read through verse 6. In these verses we will learn the difference between the mind of the flesh and the mind of the Spirit.

> Romans 8:3-6: *3 For God has done what the Law could not do, [its power] being weakened by the flesh [the entire nature of man without the Holy Spirit]. Sending His own Son in the guise of sinful flesh and as an offering for sin, [God] condemned sin in the flesh [subdued, overcame, <u>deprived it of its power over all who accept that sacrifice</u>]. 4 So that the righteous and just requirement of the Law might be fully met in us who live and move not in the ways of the flesh but in the ways of the Spirit [our lives governed not by the standards and according to the dictates of the flesh, but controlled by the Holy Spirit]. 5 For those who are according to the flesh and are controlled by its unholy desires <u>set their minds on</u> and pursue those things which gratify <u>the flesh</u>, but those who are according to the Spirit and are controlled by the desires of the Spirit <u>set their minds on</u> and seek those things which gratify <u>the [Holy] Spirit.</u> 6 Now the mind of the flesh [which is sense and reason without the Holy Spirit] is death [death that comprises all the miseries arising from sin, both here and hereafter]. But the mind of the [Holy] Spirit is life and [soul] peace [both now and forever]. AMP*

What did God do so that we could live free from sin's power to condemn us? (Verse 3)

____

Who will experience this freedom? (Verse 3)

____

When a person is walking according to the flesh, what is their mind focused on? (verse 5)

____

When a person is walking according the Spirit, what is their mind focused on? (verse 5)

____

What is the mind of the flesh, and what does it produce in your life? (verse 6)

When your mind is focused on Jesus, what does it produce in your life? (verse 6)

Sin loses it's power when you accept Jesus' sacrifice

Romans 8:3 explains that our Father God did for us what the law could never do. The law could never make us righteous because our flesh was too weak to keep it perfectly. So our loving Father sent Jesus to be a sacrifice for our sins. When we accept what His sacrifice provided for us, sin loses it's power to condemn us! So what did Jesus' sacrifice provide for you and I?

> Hebrews 10:12,14 says, *"But our High Priest offered himself to God as a single sacrifice for sins, good for all time. Then he sat down in the place of honor at God's right hand. 14 For by that one offering he forever made perfect those who are being made holy. NLT*

So, what did Jesus' one sacrifice do for you? (verse 14)

Jesus' one sacrifice completely removed the guilt and shame of your failures by giving you a brand new identity. His one sacrifice made you holy, perfect, and without fault in His sight forever! Because of Jesus, there is nothing wrong or lacking in you. So how do you actually experience this freedom from guilt and shame? When you accept the truth that Jesus' one sacrifice made you perfectly righteous, perfectly qualified, and perfectly approved, your failures and your negative circumstances have no more power to condemn you.

Live according to the dictates of the Spirit

Romans 8:4 tells us that the righteous requirements of the law are met in us when we live not according to the dictates of our flesh, but according to the dictates of the Spirit. In other words, we see ourselves as perfectly righteous and qualified in Jesus when we quit listening to the voice of condemnation and begin listening to the voice of righteousness.

The word *mind* in Romans 8:5 comes from the Greek word *phroneo* (G5426 Strong's) which means "to exercise the mind, that is, entertain or have an opinion; think".

- The mind of the flesh thinks on its own opinion of a situation, and depends on its own ability, which produces death (Galatians 5:19-21)

- The mind of the Spirit listens to and thinks upon God's opinion of a situation and depends on His Spirit within them which produces life and peace (Galatians 5:22-25)

So how do we distinguish between the mind of the flesh and the mind of the Spirit? Let's take a look at how they would look in the area of relationships. Let's say you are having a struggle because you are irritated with someone in your life. The mind of the flesh thinks thoughts like these: "Why did they act like that? I cannot believe they said those hurtful things to me. I think I'll just stop talking to them for a while; they might hurt me again, so I'm just going to protect myself." Thoughts like these produce anger, offense, resentment, and division toward the person. This is what happens when you take on your own opinion of the person and the situation instead of God's. Now, having thoughts like these does not mean you are not a born-again, loved, righteous, child of God. It just means that you have your mind on your own opinion of the situation, instead of God's. But that is not where you want to live, because it only produces death. So, let's refocus.

Now, the same situation, only this time your mind is on the Spirit. This same person has irritated you and you are tempted to be offended and angry toward them. Instead of remaining occupied by the flesh, you turn your thoughts to Jesus and say, "Lord, I know You love me. Empower me to see this person through Your eyes. Help me to love them, Lord, because Your love lives in me. Create in me the desire and power to do what pleases You." Now your mind is focused on Jesus, and guess what that produces? Peace and love. All of a sudden, not by your own work, not by your own trying and effort, but by the Spirit, your heart begins to change toward that person. You are living and walking in the *Spirit.*

Here's one more example. The other day I had plans to get quite a bit done, but by the end of the day, my stack of things to do was piled higher than it was at the beginning. Because I hadn't accomplished much, these kind of thoughts were running through my head, "I can't do this; this is just too hard. I want to quit." I felt really inadequate. The funny thing is that only a few days earlier I told my friends, "I love everything about what I do!" but now I was thinking, "I want to fire myself. Can I please just go home?" What was coming up in my heart was death, discouragement and inadequacy. In short I was experiencing a condemned mind. And then, I took a moment to get away with Jesus. "Lord, I need You. I'm feeling so weak, tired, and incapable. Remind me of who I am. Help me see Your opinion. Help me to see the truth again, Lord." And of course, He started reminding me, "Connie, I love you. I've equipped you with everything you need to carry out My will. I strengthen and empower you. It's not you doing it, it's Me working through you." I agreed with Him, "That's right, Lord. You are my Strength. You work in me to do Your will." In no time, I was back in the Spirit, saying, "Woo hoo! I have places to go, and things to do! Let's get on with it! The Spirit of God is working and living and empowering me!" So, what happened? I refocused. Where my mind had been filled with thoughts of death, now it was full of life. Do you see the difference? Your opinion will produce death; His opinion will produce life. When we refocus our thoughts on Jesus, we begin to experience His peace in our soul.

Let's read this same passage of Scripture in the Message Bible:

> Romans 8:4-7: *"And now what the law code asked for but we couldn't deliver is accomplished as we, instead of redoubling our own efforts, simply embrace what the Spirit is doing in us. 5 Those who think they can do it on their own end up obsessed with measuring their own moral muscle but never get around to exercising it in real life. Those who trust God's action in them find that God's Spirit is in them—living and breathing God! 6 Obsession with self in these matters is a dead end; attention to God leads us out into the open, into a spacious, free life. 7 Focusing on the self is the opposite of focusing on God. MSG*

According to this passage of Scripture, explain the two different ways to live.

___

___

___

The Apostle Paul here describes what it looks like to have the mind of the Spirit. As we really begin to embrace how much we are loved, and accept Jesus' sacrifice on our behalf, that's when peace, joy and the ability to truly love people come out in our lives. What the law could never do for us, the Spirit produces in us. When you are occupied with your flesh and your own ability, it can only produce death, and we have all experienced death in our hearts. Being self-focused produces the works of the flesh in our lives. These works are negative emotions like fear, anxiety, stress, resentment, offense, unforgiveness, anger, and frustration.

Jesus came for us to have abundant life. He came for us to live a different way. When we are focused on Jesus, the fruit of the Spirit comes out. That's why grace is so amazing, not because it gives us the freedom to "live in sin and God will still love us", but because it produces fruit in our lives, simply by embracing Jesus' one sacrifice. When we simply embrace that we are already righteous, perfect, and qualified because of Him, faith, love, peace, and joy manifests in our lives. Any time you hear the enemy tell you, "You can't do it; you're a failure. It's never going to work out for you," just refocus on Jesus and say, "Jesus, Your one sacrifice made me perfect. There's nothing wrong with me. I'm qualified in You, Lord. You love me."

I don't just want to be told that I am "positionally" righteous, I want to experience the fruit of righteousness in my life. I want the abundant life that Jesus died to give me to manifest in my life. Do you feel that way too?

Romans 8:6 tells us how we can experience this abundant life Jesus came to give us. It says that when our mind is focused on the flesh it produces death and misery in our soul, but when our mind is focused on the Spirit it produces life and peace in our soul.

The fruit of a person's life whose mind is on the Flesh

> Galatians 5:18-21 *18 But if you are guided (led) by the [Holy] Spirit, you are not subject to the Law. 19 Now the doings (practices) of the flesh are clear (obvious): they are immorality, impurity, indecency, 20 Idolatry, sorcery, enmity, strife, jealousy, anger (ill temper), selfishness, divisions (dissensions), party spirit (factions, sects with peculiar opinions, heresies), 21 Envy, drunkenness, carousing, and the like. I warn you beforehand, just as I did previously, that those who do such things shall not inherit the kingdom of God. AMP*

These verses reveal what a mind focused on the flesh will produce in our lives. When we rely on ourselves and our own opinion, it produces death in our soul and we will not experience peace, joy and the fruit of righteousness in our lives. Even though we are a new creation in Jesus because our minds are occupied with ourselves, selfishness, jealousy, strife, and anger are the result. This is not who we are on the inside, but it is the result of relying upon our flesh instead of Jesus.

The fruit of a person's life whose mind is on the Spirit

> Galatians 5:22-25 *22 But the fruit of the [Holy] Spirit [the work which His presence within accomplishes] is love, joy (gladness), peace, patience(an even temper, forbearance), kindness, goodness (benevolence), faithfulness, 23 Gentleness (meekness, humility), self-control (self-restraint, continence). Against such things there is no law [that can bring a charge]. 24 And those who belong to Christ Jesus (the Messiah) have crucified the flesh (the godless human nature) with its passions and appetites and desires. 25 If we live by the [Holy] Spirit, let us also walk by the Spirit. [If by the Holy Spirit we have our life in God, let us go forward walking in line, our conduct controlled by the Spirit.] AMP.*

These verses reveal what your life will produce when your mind is focused on the Spirit. When you refocus your thoughts on Jesus and accept His sacrifice that made you holy, righteous and good, the fruit of righteousness will manifest in your life. I love how this passage of Scripture brings out that it is His presence within us that accomplishes this and not our own effort or strength. When your mind is on the Spirit, you are constantly looking to Jesus and His strength to produce good fruit in your life. You are letting Jesus live His life through you.

What is the difference between the mind of the flesh and the mind of the Spirit?

____

How will you apply what you learned in this lesson to your own life?"

____

____

____

You Live in the Spirit

Romans 8:7-14

Take time to pray before you begin.

Today we will look at the difference between being "in the flesh" and being "in the Spirit." We will read Romans 8:7-14 in the King James Version to get the best understanding of what is being taught in these verses. In Romans 8:1-6, the Apostle Paul clearly showed us the difference between the mind of the flesh and the mind of the Spirit. Then in verse 9, He reminds us that we are "in the Spirit." Often we can get down on ourselves because we allowed our minds to wander away from Jesus and dwell on the flesh, but all we need when that happens to us is to be reminded of our true identity. The real you has the mind of Christ. The real you has the Spirit of the living God dwelling in you. You are in the Spirit because you belong to Jesus!

> Romans 8:7-14: *7 Because the carnal mind is enmity against God: for it is not subject to the law of God, neither indeed can be. 8 So then they that are in the flesh cannot please God. 9 <u>But ye are not in the flesh, but in the Spirit,</u> if so be that the Spirit of God dwell in you. Now if any man have not the Spirit of Christ, he is none of his. 10 And if Christ be in you, the body is dead because of sin; but the Spirit is life because of righteousness. 11 But if the Spirit of him that raised up Jesus from the dead dwell in you, he that raised up Christ from the dead shall also quicken your mortal bodies by his Spirit that dwelleth in you. 12 Therefore, brethren, we are debtors, not to the flesh, to live after the flesh. 13 For if ye live after the flesh, ye shall die: but if ye through the Spirit do mortify the deeds of the body, ye shall live. 14 For as many as are led by the Spirit of God, they are the sons of God. KJV*

What does verse 7 teach us about the carnal mind?

____

____

What does verse 8 say about those who are "in the flesh?"

____

____

Day 3

What does the Apostle Paul remind you of concerning your identity in Christ in verse 9? Are you "in the flesh" or "in the Spirit?"

____

If Jesus lives in you and the Spirit that raised Him from the dead dwells in you, what is true about you according to verses 10 and 11?

____

____

What is the result of living "after the flesh?" (verse 13)

____

____

What is true about you? (verse 14)

____

____

Now let's study this passage of Scripture verse by verse for clarity and deeper understanding of the truth being taught.

Verse 7: The "carnal mind" is a mind that is not in agreement with God. Enmity means to be opposed to God. Those who have the Spirit of God in them agree that the law of God is holy, just and good. Even though we have failed to keep it at times, we still agree that living according to God's Word is what is right.

Verse 8: In this verse we see that those who are "in the flesh" cannot please God. You are either "in the Spirit" because you have placed your faith in Christ or you are "in the flesh" because you have not received what Jesus did for you on the cross.

Verse 9: The Apostle Paul reminds us in this verse that if Jesus lives in you, you are not "in the flesh." We don't have to wonder, "Am I in the flesh or in the Spirit? Am I pleasing to God or do I displease Him?" We are "in the Spirit" because Christ lives in us! You are pleasing to God because you have placed your faith in Jesus!

In Romans 8:7-14, the Apostle Paul made a clear distinction between being "in" the flesh and "living after" the flesh. In verses 8 and 9, the word that was translated "in" is the Greek word *en*, and it denotes a "(fixed) position (in place, time or state)" (Strong's Concordance). In contrast, the word that was translated "after" in Romans 8:12-13 denotes "according to anything as a standard, agreeably to" (Thayer's Greek-English Lexicon). Therefore, when Paul spoke of being "in" the flesh or Spirit, he was referring to a fixed position or state of being. When he spoke of being "after" the flesh or Spirit, he was referring to whatever we are agreeing with at any given time. Therefore, a Christian can be living after the flesh by not agreeing with God's opinion of themselves or others, but their position in Christ and their true identity remains the same.

Verses 10 and 11: These verses explain that if Christ lives in you, you have a new life.

Before you placed your faith in Jesus, death came to your body because of sin and guilt, but now the same Spirit that raised Jesus from the dead dwells in you and gives life to your mortal body through the gift of righteousness.

The word "life" in this verse comes from the Greek word, *zoe* which means "the very life of God." (Strong's). His life includes love, health, prosperity, peace, and joy. The Spirit brings life to our body, which includes our mind. That means the Spirit brings health, strength, vitality, peace and prosperity to our minds, freeing us from all guilt, shame, condemnation, depression, anxiety or fear. As you occupy yourself with Jesus and your identity in Him, life is restored to your mind, and God's grace reigns in your life through righteousness.

When you live after the dictates of the flesh (listening to the voice of condemnation), it affects your mind and body in a negative way, but when you live after the dictates of the Spirit (listening to the voice of righteousness), the Spirit of God brings life to your mortal body!

> We see this truth again in Proverbs 4:20-22: *20 My son, give attention to my words; incline your ear to my sayings. 21 Do not let them depart from your eyes; Keep them in the midst of your heart; 22 For they are life to those who find them, And health to all their flesh. NKJV*

What will bring life and health to all your flesh?

Verses 12-14: You were not created to live after the flesh, occupying your mind with the voice of condemnation. You were created to live after the Spirit, occupying your mind with the voice of righteousness. Condemnation kills, but the Spirit brings life by reminding us of who we are in Jesus and empowering us to bear the fruit of righteousness. The Spirit of God leads us into a life of peace, joy, love, confidence, and security. You are led by God's Spirit because you are a child of God!

> Let's read Romans 8:11-14 in the Message Bible: *"It stands to reason, doesn't it, that if the alive-and-present God who raised Jesus from the dead moves into your life, he'll do the same thing in you that he did in Jesus, bringing you alive to himself? When God lives and breathes in you (and he does, as surely as he did in Jesus), you are delivered from that dead life. With his Spirit living in you, your body will be as alive as Christ's! 12 So don't you see that we don't owe this old do-it-yourself life one red cent. 13 There's nothing in it for us, nothing at all. The best thing to do is give it a decent burial and get on with your new life. 14 God's Spirit beckons. There are things to do and places to go!*

So, Awake to Righteousness!

Give the do-it-yourself life a decent burial and get on with the life God has called you to live. You are free from condemnation because you are in Christ Jesus! So occupy your

Day 3

mind with Jesus, and listen to the voice of righteousness. The same spirit that raised Jesus from the dead lives in you and gives life to your mind and body! You've been made a righteous child of God, and you are led by His Spirit!

What did you learn from today's lesson and how will you apply it to your life?

Who's Your Daddy?

Romans 8:15-28

Day 1

No Longer a Fearful Slave, but a Beloved Son

Day 2

God's Glory Revealed in You!

Day 3

All Things Work Together for Your Good

No Longer a Fearful Slave, but a Beloved Son

Romans 8:15-17

Take time to pray before you begin.

In Romans chapter 7 you learned that you are married to the perfect husband, Jesus. Now in Romans chapter 8 you will learn that you also have the perfect Daddy.

Read Romans 8:15-17: *15 For [the Spirit which] you have now received [is] not a spirit of slavery to put you once more in bondage to fear, but you have received the Spirit of adoption [the Spirit producing sonship] in [the bliss of] which we cry, Abba Father! 16 The Spirit Himself [thus] testifies together with our own spirit, [assuring us] that we are children of God. 17 And if we are [His] children, then we are [His] heirs also: heirs of God and fellow heirs with Christ [sharing His inheritance with Him]; only we must share His suffering if we are to share His glory. AMP*

Let's read these verses again in the New Living Translation:

15 So you have not received a spirit that makes you fearful slaves. Instead, you received God's Spirit when he adopted you as his own children. Now we call him, "Abba, Father." 16 For his Spirit joins with our spirit to affirm that we are God's children. 17 And since we are his children, we are his heirs. In fact, together with Christ we are heirs of God's glory. But if we are to share his glory, we must also share his suffering.

What kind of spirit have you received? (verse 15)

____

Now that you are God's child, what do you call Him? (verse 15)

____

As a child of God, what is your inheritance? (verse 17)

____

Now let's study each verse in Romans 8:15-17.

Verse 15: When you think you have to live up to a certain standard to earn God's blessing and His approval, you live as a fearful slave to the law. The Bible says that the law condemns (2 Corinthians 3:6). It produces a condemned mindset and puts you in bondage to fear. But you were set free from the slavery of the law when Jesus came to buy your freedom.

Galatians 4:4-7 says, *4 But when the right time came, God sent his Son, born of a woman, subject to the law. 5 God sent him to buy freedom for us who were slaves to the law, so that he could adopt us as his very own children. 6 And because we are his children, God has sent the Spirit of his Son into our hearts, prompting us to call out, "Abba, Father." 7 Now you are no longer a slave but God's own child. And since you are his child, God has made you his heir. NLT*

When you were a slave to the law, why did your Heavenly Father send Jesus to buy your freedom? (verse 5)

What does God's Spirit prompt you to call Him? (verse 6)

What is true of you since you are no longer a slave to the law? What is your new identity and your inheritance in Jesus? (verse 7)

The Difference between the spirit of slavery and the spirit of adoption

A **slave** serves his master to earn his wages, but lives with the constant fear of punishment or disapproval if he does something wrong.

A **son** receives an inheritance of everything that belongs to His Father simply because he is His child. He does not earn it; it is a gift given not as a result of his own work, but as a result of the work of his Father. The Father's perfect love for the son casts out all fear. (1 John 4:18)

This passage of Scripture reveals that at one time we were all fearful slaves to the law. As I pondered on this truth, the story of the children of Israel enslaved in Egypt came to my mind. They worked so hard under the taskmaster of rules and barely survived. Every day they struggled to get their work done so they could earn a portion of their master's goods. They lived like fearful slaves. But then one day Moses came to set God's people free from the taskmaster of the law so they could enjoy the inheritance of the Promised Land.

This is true of all of us in a spiritual sense. We were all under the taskmaster of the law, trying to be good enough, but always feeling like we came up short. But then Jesus came to free us from the fearful slave mentality by purchasing us with His own blood. Your Heavenly Father loved you so much that He sent Jesus to buy your freedom from the slavery to the law so that He could adopt you as His very own child. You received Jesus' identity and just like Him, you were made a son of God. Jesus is your promised land! You are no longer a fearful slave, but a beloved child of the King of kings!

I used to live like a fearful slave even though I am a beloved child of God. The Bible says that God's people perish for lack of knowledge because they don't know their true identity. That was true of me at one time. Instead of resting in the truth that Jesus had qualified me and I was a joint heir with Him, I tried to qualify myself for God's blessings by my good works. This produced a fearful slave mentality in me and put me in bondage to the law. Fear is the predominant symptom of the life of a Christian who lives their lives in bondage to the law (Romans 8:15). Fear of things not working out well, fear of what others think, fear of disapproval and rejection, fear concerning finances, fear of sickness, concerns for my children were some of the fears I experienced because I did not know my true identity.

But when I began to understand that I was no longer a fearful slave to the law and I began to awake to the truth that I was a beloved child of the King of kings and an heir to all that He is and all that He has, I began to experience a peace and joy that I had never experienced before in my Christian life. The devil had deceived me for too long, but now I understood the truth that set me free! I will never go back to living like a slave in Egypt, living under the heavy burden of trying to be good enough to earn something that already belongs to me in Jesus! Jesus is my promised land! And I have discovered who my Daddy is!

Abba, Father

Romans 5:15-16 and Galatians 4:6 show that you have not received a spirit of slavery that put you in bondage to fear, but you have received the spirit of sonship. God sent the spirit of His Son into your heart, prompting you to call Him, *Abba*, Father. God's Spirit in you assures you that you are a child of God!

Abba is the Aramaic equivalent to our modern day word "daddy." It implies intimacy with and complete dependence on the One who loves you and takes care of you. As a child you were completely dependent on your parents to provide love, food, clothing, and shelter for you. You didn't think, "Oh, I've got to take care of myself." You were simply a child who was provided for and taken care of. That's the kind of relationship your Heavenly Father wants to have with you.

We all desire to have a Daddy that loves us. We all have a need inside our hearts to have a Daddy who approves of us, a Daddy that's proud of us, a Daddy that delights in us. Have you ever thought of God as your Daddy? Your natural father may have made you feel like you were never good enough, he may have been hard on you, or maybe even abandoned you, but no matter what kind of natural father you had in this life, you have a new Father now. He is a perfect Father. He is the kind of Daddy you've always wanted!

- He only sees good in you because of Jesus (Ephesians 1:3,4; 2 Corinthians 5:21)!
- When you fail, He will never be angry with you and punish you (Isaiah 54:9-10)!
- He corrects you by reminding you of who you are and how much you are loved! (Luke 15:20-24)
- He will never leave you or forsake you (Hebrews 13:5)

- Everything He is and has belongs to you: Provision, wisdom, power, prosperity, health, love, peace, joy, kindness, goodness, power, grace, mercy.
- Every good and perfect gift comes down from your Daddy. (James 1:17)
- Zephaniah 3:17 says that your Daddy takes delight in you with gladness. He doesn't even mention your past sins or even recall them. And with His love, He will calm all your fears. He rejoices over you with joyful songs. You are the delight of His heart; His precious son or daughter and He is so proud of you!
- You have His complete approval (Ephesians 1:6). He pours His blessing into your life just because you are His beloved child! That's the character of your Abba Father. When you live conscious of His great love for you, peace will be the fruit of your life!

You are a joint heir with Jesus!

Romans 8:17 assures you that if you are God's child, then you are His heir and everything He has belongs to you. As you awake to your sonship, you'll quit trying to earn God's blessings and rest in the truth that you are already an heir. You don't have to earn anything because Jesus already earned it for you! Because of His perfect obedience, He fulfilled the Law and inherited everything that belongs to the Father. You are now a joint heir with Jesus! Simply by putting your trust in Jesus, you became an heir to the glory of God!

> Romans 8:17 assures you that if you are God's child, then you are His heir and everything He has belongs to you. As you awake to your sonship, you'll quit trying to earn God's blessings and rest in the truth that you are already an heir.

My husband and I have four children. When we pass away, they will inherit everything we own. Now there are times when they disobey us and don't do exactly what we would like them to. But they are still our heirs. They didn't earn their status by perfectly obeying every rule my husband and I gave them. And they certainly didn't earn what we own. So, how do they get in on this inheritance? Simply because they are our children and we love them. They don't have to earn it, or deserve it, they just receive it because they are heirs of everything that we have.

That's the way it is with our Daddy, God. We don't earn or deserve any of His blessings. We have been made worthy simply because we are His children. We've not been given a spirit of slavery that puts us in bondage to fear, but we have been given the spirit of adoption by which we cry out, "Abba, Father!"

Who's Your Daddy?

Not too long ago I was talking to a pastor's wife who is a friend of mine, and she confided in me that her husband was getting ready to make some important financial decisions. I shared with her that she doesn't have to worry because she has a Father who loves her and has promised to lead them and provide all their needs. I reminded her that they are blessed because of Jesus and encouraged her to remember who they are in Him! Afterwards, she went home and shared what we spoke about with her husband. She encouraged him by saying, "We don't have to worry about this. We can trust the Father because He loves us, and He's going to take care of us." After her conversation with her husband, she came back to me and said, "Connie, I shared what you said with my husband, and we came up with this saying, "Who's your Daddy?" Now, every time he asks me "What are we going to do?" I say, "Who's your Daddy?" And every time I say, "What are we going to do if this doesn't work out?" He reminds me, "Who's your Daddy?" I thought, "Wow! What a great way to renew your mind when you're tempted to be worried or fearful about something!"

So when you find yourself feeling fearful, ask yourself, "Who's my Daddy?" When you wake up to the truth that you are no longer a fearful slave, but a beloved child of God, you will no longer live in bondage to fear. That's not to say that you will never be tempted, but for you there will always be an escape. Just cry out, "Abba, Father, You love me and I know You are going to take care of everything that concerns me!" Share your concerns with Him, and rest in His unfailing love! You have the perfect Daddy and you can trust Him because He loves you with all His heart! You are a beloved child of the King of kings — you can live fearless in this world!

Take some time right now to answer this question for yourself, "Who's your Daddy?"

How does knowing this bring peace to your heart?

God's Glory Revealed in You!

Romans 8:17-25

Take time to pray before you begin.

Today we will move on in our study of Romans Chapter 8 and continue to learn that we are beloved children of God and heirs of His glory.

> Romans 8:17-18: *17 And if we are [His] children, then we are [His] heirs also: heirs of God and fellow heirs with Christ [sharing His inheritance with Him]; only we must share His suffering if we are to share His glory. 18 [But what of that?] For I consider that the sufferings of this present time (this present life) are not worth being compared with the glory that is about to be revealed to us and in us and for us and conferred on us! AMP*

As children of God, what two things do we share with Jesus? (verse 17)

____

____

Which of these two things will far exceed the other? What can we enjoy experiencing as a child of God? (verse 18)

____

We will take a deeper look into the meanings of the words *suffering* and *glory* to get a better understanding of the truth being taught in these verses.

The word *suffering* in verse 17 is often misunderstood. It comes from the Greek word *sumpascho* (Strong's 4841) which means "to experience pain jointly or of the same kind (specifically persecution)." It is specifically the word "persecutions."

Some people have read the word *suffering* in the Bible and interpreted it as sickness, poverty, or tragedy in life, but this is not what this word means at all. It literally means "persecutions for righteousness sake." It is people coming against you because of your identification with Jesus.

The word *glory* in verse 17 comes from the Greek word *doxa* and it "primarily signifies an opinion, the honor resulting from a good opinion. It is used of the nature and acts of God in self-manifestation of what He essentially is and does; the word denotes the manifested perfection of His character, especially His righteousness." *[Vines New Testament]*

With these definitions in mind, we can see that these verses literally mean that if we are joint heirs with Jesus, we will share the same persecutions He received as a result of Him sharing the glory of His Father. In other words, if we live in the good opinion of our Heavenly Father and declare, as Jesus did, that we are His beloved children, then we will also share the persecutions that Jesus received from the religious people of his day, and the world.

> In Matthew 5:10-12, Jesus said, *"10 Blessed and happy and enviably fortunate and spiritually prosperous (in the state in which the born-again child of God enjoys and finds satisfaction in God's favor and salvation, regardless of his outward conditions) are those who are persecuted for righteousness' sake (for being and doing right), for theirs is the kingdom of heaven! 11 Blessed (happy, to be envied, and spiritually prosperous—with life-joy and satisfaction in God's favor and salvation, regardless of your outward conditions) are you when people revile you and persecute you and say all kinds of evil things against you falsely on My account. 12 Be glad and supremely joyful, for your reward in heaven is great (strong and intense), for in this same way people persecuted the prophets who were before you."* AMP

What were the sufferings that Jesus said you would experience on His account? (verse 11)

____

What promise does He give those who are persecuted because of their identity with Him? (verses 11 and 12)

____

Jesus received persecutions from others because of His confident belief and declaration that He was the beloved Son of God, and one with His Father. As we receive this truth as well, we too will receive persecutions from those who live under the law and think you have to earn God's blessing and approval! When you truly take a stand for Jesus and declare that it is all about what He has done and not about what we do, some people will say evil things about you. Religious people will call you a heretic in the very same way they did Jesus. You may find yourself being persecuted for identifying completely with Jesus and your oneness with Him.

But the Good News is revealed in Romans 8:18. This verse says that the persecutions you receive in this life will not even come close to comparing to the glory of God that will be revealed in and through you as you keep your eyes on Jesus! You will be a living testimony of God's love and goodness as His good opinion of you is manifested in your life for the whole world to see!

When I began to teach that the Good News is all about what Jesus did, and not what we have to do, I began to get persecuted. People who hadn't heard the Good News — that you are righteous and blessed, not because of your good works, but because of the finished work of Jesus — began to say evil things about me. They had been taught, "You have to qualify yourself for God's blessing through your tithing and giving, and faithfulness to God," and they didn't like that I was taking the glory away from their "good works" and giving all the glory to Jesus!

The law is a way to control and manipulate people through fear to get them to do what you want them to do. That's why religious people like the law. When I began to teach God's people that Jesus fulfilled the law for us and made us righteous by faith in Him, they realized that they were free to be led and controlled by the Spirit of God instead of by man. That's when some people began to say negative things about me and what I was teaching.

At first this disturbed my heart, so I went and talked to my Heavenly Father about it. I asked Him, "Father, what do You have to say about this? People are saying these evil things about me." And He reminded me of the Scripture in Romans 8:18. Through this verse I heard Him speak to my heart, "Connie, the persecutions that you are receiving now are nothing compared to the glory that's going to be revealed in you, through you and all around you!" My heart leapt with joy! All of a sudden I realized that yes, there would be religious people who would come against me, reject me, and say evil things about me because I identify myself completely with Jesus, but the glory of God — the manifestation of Who He is in me and Who I am in Jesus — would far surpass any persecution I would endure. God would use me to bring His truth and the understanding of "Christ in you, the hope of glory" to a hurting world. And the people who have received this truth have experienced life transformation as they too, are seeing the glory of God manifest in their lives!

> ...the Good News is revealed in Romans 8:18. This verse says that the persecutions you receive in this life will not even come close to comparing to the glory of God that will be revealed in and through you as you keep your eyes on Jesus!

A while back, I got a long derogatory email, which in summary said, "What makes you think you can teach the Bible? You are not qualified and you shouldn't be teaching anyone." After reading it, I thought, "It doesn't matter what her opinion is of me. The only thing that matters is what my Daddy says. He is the final authority in my life, and He says I'm anointed and qualified to preach the Good News and to set the captives free because Jesus lives in me! That's all the qualification I need." As I renewed my mind to that truth, my heart was filled with peace as I agreed with my Father's good opinion of me.

When you start realizing that you are wonderful, blessed, anointed, and qualified because of Jesus, those "older brothers" are not going to like it. They are the ones who have been working hard their whole lives and trying their best to be good. So they don't like it when you come along and say "I'm blessed because of Jesus." They may be a family member, a child, a parent, a friend, or even your own spouse. But the persecutions that you receive because you are identifying with Jesus and what He did for you, are nothing compared to the glory that will be revealed in and through you for all the world to see!

Now that you are awake to righteousness, you know that you are an heir, a daughter or son of God, and you bring life to everyone around you because you share the Good News. You tell them, "You don't have to work so hard. You are loved and blessed. Your Daddy loves you and you are His heir. Just let yourself be loved." Everyone wants a Daddy who loves and approves of them, One who gives them everything, just because they are His. This is the Good News of the Gospel that sets people free.

The sufferings, persecutions, and negative words that come at us because we stand for truth were suffered by Jesus in the same way. He was persecuted; He was reviled. It says that people "said all manner of evil against Him," just because He said, "I am the Beloved Son of God," The religious people didn't like what He had to say. He stood for who He was and declared what the Father said about Him, which didn't make some of the people around Him happy. When you start declaring what the Father says about you, there are going to be some that don't like what you are saying, either. But don't concern yourself with that, because His glory is going to manifest in your life, and all around you. The few persecutions that may come your way won't compare to the wonderful things ahead. I have witnessed this in my own life, and now I get letters, emails, and people coming up to me all the time, telling me how their lives are being transformed by the ministry of Because of Jesus. And it's because of the Good News that it's all about Jesus, and that they've been made righteous as a free gift. And every time I hear these wonderful testimonies, the glory far outweighs any of the negative things I may hear. So, don't be afraid of what people think, because you stand for the truth. You're not a fearful slave to the negative opinions of others. You are an heir of the Father's good opinion of you. Your Daddy is fully pleased, because you have put your faith in Jesus.

> Now let's read Romans 8:19-25: *19 For [even the whole] creation (all nature) waits expectantly and longs earnestly for God's sons to be made known [waits for the revealing, the disclosing of their sonship]. 20 For the creation (nature) was subjected to frailty (to futility, condemned to frustration), not because of some intentional fault on its part, but by the will of Him Who so subjected it—[yet] with the hope 21 That nature (creation) itself will be set free from its bondage to decay and corruption [and gain an entrance] into the glorious freedom of God's children. 22 We know that the whole creation [of irrational creatures] has been moaning together in the pains of labor until now. 23 And not only the creation, but we ourselves too, who have and enjoy the firstfruits of the [Holy] Spirit [a foretaste of the blissful things to come] groan inwardly as we wait for the redemption of our bodies. 24 For in [this] hope we were saved. But hope [the object of] which is seen is not hope. For how can one hope for what he already sees? 25 But if we hope for what is still unseen by us, we wait for it with patience and composure. AMP*

Verse 19: All of creation is waiting for God's sons to realize who they truly are. It waits for them to take their position in the Kingdom of God. As they declare that what their Daddy says about them is true, His glory will manifest in the earth!

Verses 20-22: Because of the curse that sin brought into the world, all of creation was subject to corruption. But with eager anticipation, all creation waits for the day that it will join God's children in glorious freedom from death and decay. At Christ's return the earth will be redeemed and never be subject to death and decay again.

Verses 23-25: As children of God, His glory is our inheritance. We can enjoy the manifestation of God's goodness in our lives every day. Our spirits have eternal life and we will never truly die. Yet, we live in a body that will eventually die and decay, but the real us will live on forever! Our full redemption includes a new body that will never grow old and die. We will be given a body just like Jesus received when He rose again from the dead. We will live young, healthy, vibrant and full of energy for all eternity! This is our future hope of glory!

What did the Holy Spirit reveal to your heart about the glory of God?

All Things Work Together for Your Good

Romans 8:26-28

Take time to pray before you begin.

As a child of God, we have the promise of the Holy Spirit to help and strengthen us in every situation of our lives. Today we will study Romans 8:26-28 and be encouraged by the truth that as heirs of God's glory all things work together for our good.

> Romans 8:26-28: *26 So too the [Holy] Spirit comes to our aid and bears us up in our weakness; for we do not know what prayer to offer nor how to offer it worthily as we ought, but the Spirit Himself goes to meet our supplication and pleads in our behalf with unspeakable yearnings and groanings too deep for utterance. 27 And He Who searches the hearts of men knows what is in the mind of the [Holy] Spirit [what His intent is], because the Spirit intercedes and pleads [before God] in behalf of the saints according to and in harmony with God's will. 28 We are assured and know that [God being a partner in their labor] all things work together and are [fitting into a plan] for good to and for those who love God and are called according to [His] design and purpose. AMP*

What does the Holy Spirit do for us when we feel weak and are unsure of how to pray? (verse 26)

____

____

How does the Holy Spirit intercede for us? (verse 27)

____

What can we be confident and sure of in every situation? (verse 28)

____

Verse 26: The Holy Spirit was sent to be our helper, our counselor and our guide in this world. When we are unsure about how to pray about a situation, the Spirit of God is within us to strengthen us in our weakness and help us pray the perfect will of God for our lives or the lives of those we love.

Verse 27: says that the Holy Spirit actually intercedes and pleads before God on our behalf in harmony with God's will.

Verse 28: Here we see a promise that can bring peace to your heart no matter what negative situation you may be facing. Since we know our Daddy loves us and that His will for our lives is for good and not for evil (Jeremiah 29:11), we can be absolutely confident that He is working everything together for our good because He has called us to reflect His glory in this world.

Romans 8:28 is one of my favorite Scriptures in the Bible. I can't tell you how many times it has brought peace and comfort to my heart when I was dealing with a difficult situation in my life. When I am facing a negative circumstance, I always turn to my Father and say, "Father, what do You say about this?" On a number of occasions, the Holy Spirit has reminded me of this verse and each time I have responded by saying, "Thank You, Father, that You are working this together for my good. I trust You because I know You love me!"

Let me share a personal example with you. In June of 2009, Because of Jesus Ministries was at the end of our lease at our office space. Many of the other tenants in the complex were moving out, so I assumed I was going to get a really good deal on my next lease renewal. Instead, I got a letter saying they were going to raise my rent by about twenty percent. This concerned my heart so I asked the Father, "What do You say about this?" The Holy Spirit reminded me of Romans 8:28 and I knew that this was going to work out for my good. I said, "Father, I don't know what is going to happen, but I trust that You have a good plan for me. You are working every detail into something good." This promise brought peace to my soul and I just began to rest in the truth that my Father had it all figured out.

It was the end of June, and I put my thirty-day notice in and went out of town to visit my family for two weeks. I had to be out of that office space by July 31st, and I wasn't going to be back until July 15th, which didn't leave a whole lot of time for us to get into a new place.

The morning after I returned home from my trip, I got up with a smile on my face. I was going out driving with my Daddy God, and He was going to show me where our next move would be. So, I drove around that day, just talking to the Lord, saying, "Thank You, Father, for leading and guiding me. I'm led by Your Spirit. You cause my thoughts to be agreeable to Your will. You love me, Father, and You're going to show me where You'd have us go." During the course of that day and throughout the next week, I did look at a couple of office spaces, but knew they weren't the ones. By the end of the week, my heart was leaning towards purchasing property for Because of Jesus Ministries instead of renting space.

Now at this point, I only had one week left to get us out of our present office space and into something new. So, I got a realtor, and she took me out to look at a couple of properties. During our Sunday Night home group, I told several of our friends, "You know what? I really feel like the Lord is leading us to purchase some space for the ministry." In response my friend Shannan asked, "What day do you have to be out of your current space?" And I said, "This Friday." With a bewildered look on her face she said, "What are you going to do with all the office furniture while you wait to close on the property? Do you realize that it takes at least thirty days to close on a property and that's if you have cash?" Because I had such a perfect peace in my heart it never even occurred to me that I would need to move the furniture anywhere except into the property we would purchase. I responded, "All I know is that's the way the Father's leading me, and we're going to move the furniture into the space that we purchase." Her only response was, "Okay."

On Monday, I looked at another property which I ended up having a very good feeling about. So the next day I had several people come and look at it with me and we all agreed that this is where the ministry offices should be. But I had 3 days to get out of my current office space and purchase this property. I had such a peace because I knew that my Father God was working on my behalf. I had no idea how all of this was going to happen but I did know that my Daddy was working this out for my good.

As I talked to the current owners of this property, I found out that many years ago the woman who owned it had dedicated this property to the ministry and was thrilled to know that we would be using it to spread the Gospel. We received so much favor and they allowed us to move all our office furniture into the property on Friday. She even offered to let us use the property for free for six months. At the end of the six months, we closed on the property. We ended up having twice as much office space for half the monthly cost of our previous location. That's how the Father worked it all together for my good just as He had promised.

Let me share one more personal example of God working things together for my good. Several years ago, I had organized a Girl's Getaway Cruise for the Because of Jesus team. We were very excited to go on this trip together and had paid for it over the course of about 9 months. But on the day that we were driving to the port we got news that there were some problems with our ship and we would not be able to go to the destination that we were all looking forward to visiting. I could feel the concern and disappointment all around me, but whenever I find myself in a situation like this, I always turn my thoughts to Jesus and spend some time talking with Him.

I know that my inheritance is peace and not fear or concern so I simply asked, "Father, what do you say about all of this?" Again, Romans 8:28 came up in my heart. As I continued to talk with Him, a peace came over me and I knew something really good was going to come from all of this. I settled down into perfect peace and told my friends what I heard from the Father, "We don't have to be worried or concerned. This is all going to work together for our good." I felt the Father smile as I rested in His love.

When we arrived at the ship, I could see the concerned and upset passengers all around us. I could hear people talking about the problems we were having. But I just kept thinking, "Father, thank You for working this together for our good." I was not upset, angry, or concerned because I felt confident that something really good was going to come out of all of this. The Holy Spirit had empowered me to simply believe, so I was able to thoroughly enjoy the cruise unfazed by the challenges we were facing. With my heart filled with joy and peace, I had a wonderful time with my friends.

A couple of weeks after we returned from our trip, we all received a letter apologizing for the difficulty we had encountered on the cruise, and for not being able to visit our original destination. They offered to compensate us by giving each of us a free cruise for two. So a few months later my friends and I went on another cruise, only this time we were able to bring our spouses for free as well! Not only had this worked out for our good, but it was far beyond what I could have ever hoped or dreamed could happen. We had a fabulous time on our second cruise and I was in awe of how God's glory had manifested in this situation. Still to this day when I think about how that all worked out, the Father reminds me how we can truly live free from worry, anxiety, and frustration when we truly believe that He is working every situation together for our good.

So Awake to Righteousness!

Remember, you are not a fearful slave. You are a beloved child of God — a joint heir with Jesus to the glory of God — everything He has belongs to you! When you are tempted to worry about anything, remember that your Daddy is the King of kings! Cry out to the One who loves you and remember He is working everything together for your good!

Can you remember a time when you were dealing with a negative situation and God worked it out for your good?

How were you encouraged by today's lesson and how will you apply it in your life?

Safe and Secure in Your Daddy's Love

Romans 8:29-39

Day 1

Called, Chosen, and Made Righteous

Day 2

An Heir of His Glory

Day 3

Nothing Can Separate You from His Love

Called, Chosen, and Made Righteous

Romans 8:29-30

Take time to pray before you begin.

Last week you learned that you are no longer a fearful slave, but a beloved child of God. Your Daddy is the King of kings and you are His heir. Everything He is and has belongs to you. When you understand the character of your Heavenly Father and His goodness of heart toward you, you will live safe and secure in His love. His perfect love casts out all fear from your heart.

Secure means "to live without fear, worry, or anxiety; to be confident in someone's good opinion of you."

As a child of God you can live secure in this world, free from all fear, worry and anxiety. When you know your Abba Father's love for you, and your identity in Christ, you will run to Him every time you're tempted to be afraid and He will calm all your fears with His love.

His love for you is revealed in Jesus. Today we will continue our study of Romans chapter 8, and grow in our understanding of His great love for us that is revealed in Jesus!

> Romans 8:29-30: *29 For God knew his people in advance, and he chose them to become like his Son, so that his Son would be the firstborn among many brothers and sisters. 30 And having chosen them, he called them to come to him. And having called them, he gave them right standing with himself. And having given them right standing, he gave them his glory.* NLT

> Romans 8:30: *And those whom He thus foreordained, He also called; and those whom He called, He also justified (acquitted, made righteous)... And those whom He justified, He also glorified* AMP

Make these verses personal by embracing the truth for yourself:

> *Heavenly Father, You knew me before I was ever born, and You chose me to become like Jesus. Jesus was Your firstborn son and now I am Your child as well. You not only chose me, but You called me to come to You. And when You called me to Yourself, You made me righteous in Your sight. You love me so much that You gave me Your glory!*

Take a moment to allow this truth to penetrate deep within your heart. What does this tell you about your Abba Father's heart toward you? How does this truth bring peace to your soul?

Let's recall one more time what it means to be made righteous:

Righteous means "to be justified, innocent, free from guilt or blame."

> *It is the judicial act of God, by which he pardons all the sins of those who believe in Christ, and accounts, accepts, and treats them as righteous in the eye of the law. In addition to the pardon of sin, justification declares that all the claims of the law are satisfied. The law is not relaxed or set aside, but is declared to be fulfilled in the strictest sense; and so* ***the person justified is declared to be entitled to all the advantages and rewards arising from perfect obedience to the law*** *(Romans 5:1-10). It proceeds on the crediting to the believer by God himself of the perfect righteousness, of Jesus Christ (Romans 10:3-9). Justification is not the forgiveness of a man without righteousness, but a declaration that he possesses a righteousness which perfectly and forever satisfies the law, namely, Christ's righteousness (2 Corinthians 5:21; Romans 4:6-8). www.christiananswers.net/dictionary/justification.html:Bible Encyclopedia*

Using this definition, explain what it means that you have been declared righteous by your Abba Father. Make it personal:

Because of His great love for you, your Abba Father chose you and called you to be His child. When you put your faith in Jesus, you were given a brand new identity and He declared you righteous. Your Heavenly Father declared you innocent and free from all guilt or blame. Your Daddy looked at you with great delight and said, "You are blameless, innocent and perfect in My sight forever, My child."

In a judicial act by the King of kings, He pardoned all your sins and accepts and treats you as righteous in the eye of the law. The law was not relaxed or set aside, but was declared to be fulfilled in the strictest sense. So when your Daddy declared you righteous, He made a declaration that you were entitled to all the rewards of perfect obedience. He gave you the perfect righteousness of Jesus as a gift. It is your new identity as a child of God!

When you awake to righteousness and realize who you truly are because of Jesus, fear will lose it's power in your life. You'll finally understand that you don't have to earn your Daddy's blessings. You have His complete approval as a gift. You have been qualified for every promise and now you can simply rest secure in His love. Your Daddy — the Judge, the King of kings, the Great I Am — has declared you righteous! Nobody can take that away from you! Because you put your faith in Jesus, you stand completely qualified forever.

When we are tempted to be afraid, Romans 8: 15 tells us to cry out, "Daddy, Father!" As I thought about this truth, my youngest daughter, Victoria, came to my mind. When she was little, even though she was a Momma's girl, whenever she was afraid, she always wanted her Daddy. If there was a storm outside or if we were going to ride a roller coaster ride, she always wanted to be with her Daddy. Why? Because he was big and strong and she knew he loved her, and she felt safe in his arms. Without fail, anytime Victoria was afraid, she would cry out, "Daddy! I want my Daddy!" She felt safe and secure in her Daddy's love. And it's the same for us, as children of the Most High God. When we are afraid, when life's storms are raging, when we are facing lack, when we are worried about our children, our health, or our finances, we cry out, "Daddy Father, You love me!" Our Daddy is the One who will never leave us, never forsake us, never turn His back on us, or fail us. He is the Perfect Daddy. Let's look at some of the promises our Daddy has made to us to reassure our hearts of His love:

> Isaiah 41:10: *Fear not [there is nothing to fear], for I am with you; do not look around you in terror and be dismayed, for I am your God. I will strengthen and harden you to difficulties, yes, I will help you; yes, I will hold you up and retain you with My [victorious] right hand of rightness and justice. AMP*

What does this verse tell you about your Daddy's love for you?

____

> Hebrews 13:5: *For He [God] Himself has said, I will not in any way fail you nor give you up nor leave you without support. [I will] not, [I will] not, [I will] not in any degree leave you helpless nor forsake nor let [you] down (relax My hold on you)! [Assuredly not!] AMP*

Why can you live safe and secure in His love?

____

> Isaiah 54:9-10: *9 "Just as I swore in the time of Noah that I would never again let a flood cover the earth, so now I swear that <u>I will never again be angry and punish you</u>. 10 For the mountains may move and the hills disappear, but even then my faithful love for you will remain. My covenant of blessing will never be broken," says the <u>LORD, who has mercy on you</u>. NLT*

What does this verse reveal about your Daddy's heart toward you? How does this promise bring peace to your heart?

____

____

Your Daddy is there to help you no matter what problem you may face. He will rescue you with His victorious right hand! He will never fail you nor forsake you! And no matter what mistakes you make, He swore He would never be angry or punish you again!

At one point or another, we have all had a wrong perception of our Heavenly Father. Jesus has always been my Savior, and even though I had a relationship with Him, I didn't always understand that Jesus came to reconcile me to my Father so that I could live safe and secure in His love for me. Some have thought that Jesus is this person who shielded us from the Father's anger toward our sin. But that's not true at all! Instead, Jesus is the One who reconciled us to the Father, and presents us before Him perfect, without fault and blameless in His sight. He reconciled, redeemed, and restored us so that you and I could have an intimate relationship with the Daddy we've always dreamed of having. He is never angry with you, and in Hebrews 8:12, He states emphatically, "I will never, no never, remember your sins."

For too long, God's children have been taught to think that He's judgmental and angry, and He punishes people for their sins, but that is not at all what the Bible says. We are "in Christ," and because of the blood of Jesus, we have been made righteous, innocent, perfect, so that when our Father looks at us, He smiles. We are the delight of His heart!

Your Daddy God loves you. He called you, chose you and made you righteous so that you could feel safe and secure in His love! Whenever you feel afraid, remember who you are! You are not a fearful slave, but a beloved child of the King of kings. Cry out, Abba, Father, and watch as He rescues you from all your fears!

> Psalm 34:4: *"I prayed to the LORD, and he answered me. He freed me from all my fears." NLT*

How does knowing that you've been chosen, called, and declared righteous by your loving Heavenly Father cause you to run to Him when you are afraid?

____

____

____

____

Why can you live safe and secure in His love?

____

____

____

____

____

Day 2

An Heir of His Glory

Romans 8:17, 30-32

Take time to pray before you begin.

In Romans 8:30 yesterday you learned that you were called, chosen, and declared righteous by your Heavenly Father. Today we will study the portion of this verse that says, "He gave you His glory," and see what it means to be an heir of the glory of God.

> Romans 8:17: *And since we are his children, we are his heirs. In fact, together with Christ <u>we are heirs of God's glory</u>.*
>
> Romans 8:30-32: *30 And having chosen them, he called them to come to him. And having called them, he gave them his righteousness. And having given them his righteousness, he gave them his glory. 31 What shall we say about such wonderful things as these? If God is for us, who can ever be against us? NLT 32 He who did not withhold or spare [even] His own Son but gave Him up for us all, will He not also with Him freely and graciously give us all [other] things? AMP*

What is the wonderful Good News of the Gospel of Grace? (verse 17, 30)

____

When you read verse 31, how does this truth affect your heart and why?

____

What does Romans 8:32 assure you of? Will your Daddy withhold any good thing from you?

____

The word *glory* in verses 17 and 30 comes from the Greek word, *doxa* and it means "to render or esteem glorious; to honor; to make glorious" (G1392 Strong's).

> *"Glory" primarily signifies an opinion, the honor resulting from a good opinion. It is used of the nature and acts of God in self-manifestation of what He essentially is and does; the word denotes the manifested perfection of His character, especially His righteousness. [Vines New Testament]*

With these definitions in mind, explain what it means that your Heavenly Father gave you His glory.

____

____

These definitions of glory give us a clear understanding of what is meant by the truth that we are joint heirs with Jesus to the glory of God. When your Heavenly Father gave you His glory, He esteemed you by declaring you glorious! He honored you by giving you His very good opinion. His glory is essentially who He is and what He does. When He gave you His glory, He gave you His nature — the manifested perfection of His character, especially His righteousness! When you became one with Jesus, you shared the Father's glory with Him. Your Daddy's good opinion of you is that you are just like Him! You have His DNA! You are glorious!

The glory of God is the Father's good opinion of you!

Now look at what the Father said to Jesus when He gave Him honor and glory:

> 2 Peter 1:17: *He received honor and glory from God the Father when the voice came to him from the Majestic Glory, saying, "This is my Son, whom I love; with him I am well pleased." NIV*
>
> 2 Peter 1:17: *When he received honor and glory from God the Father. The voice from the majestic glory of God said to him, "This is my dearly loved Son, who brings me great joy." NLT*

In John 17:22, Jesus said, *"I have given them the glory you gave me, so they may be one as we are one."* If you have received the same honor and glory from the Father that Jesus received, according to 2 Peter 1:17, what is your Heavenly Father saying about you?

____

Jesus demonstrated the picture of a Son who was living safe and secure in His Father's love. He came so that we could have the same kind of relationship with the Father that He did. When others came against Him to question His identity, He responded with confidence because He was fully persuaded that what His Father said about Him was true!

> In John 8:14-15, 25-26, 54 and 55, Jesus told them, *"14 These claims are valid even though I make them about myself. For I know where I came from and where I am going, but you don't know this about me. 15 You judge me with all your human limitations…." 25 "Tell us who you are," they demanded. Jesus replied, "[I am] the one I have always claimed to be. 26…I say only what I have heard from [my Father] and he is true. 54 If I am merely boasting about myself, it doesn't count. <u>But it is my Father who says these glorious things about me….</u> 55 If I said otherwise I would be as great a liar as you. NLT [Author's Insert]*

Jesus was the firstborn among many brothers and sisters and every one of us can live with this same confidence in who we are because we are heirs of God's glory — His good opinion of us is true! If we were merely boasting about ourselves, it wouldn't mean anything, but it is our Father who says these glorious things about us! And when His opinion is all that matters — just like Jesus — we will live confident and secure in this world!

The Glory of God is the manifestation of Who God is in You!

The glory of God is also defined as the nature and character of God. It is the manifestation of all that God is and has. So in order to fully understand what it means to be an heir of His glory, you must know Who your Daddy is.

So, who is He? Your Daddy is LOVE. He is PEACE. He is JOY. He is GOODNESS. He is KINDNESS. He is SELF-CONTROL. He is HEALTH. He is WEALTH. He is PROVISION. He is RIGHTEOUS. He is PERFECT. He is VICTORIOUS. He is WISDOM. He is POWERFUL. He is STRENGTH. He is WITHOUT FAULT, He is HOLY, HE is WORTHY!

Take a moment to add your own words to this list. Who is your Daddy?

____

____

____

So if this is your Daddy's glory (His nature) and He gave His glory to you, you are just like Him. You have His nature in you! Finish these sentences with the truth of who you are as a joint heir with Jesus, of God's glory.

I am________________! I am________________! I am________________!

I am________________! I am________________! I am________________!

I am________________! I am________________! I am________________!

We are one with the Father, and one with Jesus. When you know who He is, you will know who you are! As His child, He gave you His glory! You can confidently say, "I am love. I am peaceful. I am good. I am healthy. I am prosperous. I am joyful. I am kind. I am worthy. I am holy and righteous because I am an heir of my Heavenly Father's glory!" When your Daddy looks at you, He sees Himself! You are made in His image. He adores you! You make His heart sing! (Zephaniah 3:17)

The glory of God is the *manifestation* of Who God is in you! It's the manifestation of wealth, the manifestation of health; the manifestation of peace, the manifestation of wisdom, the manifestation of guidance and favor, the manifestation of security and confidence. The glory of God is the *manifestation* of who God is.

Let's see how we can apply this to the different areas of our lives:

When symptoms of sickness come on your body, cry out, *"Daddy, Father, You love me. You are health, and I am health because I'm an heir of your glory!"*

When you are facing financial lack, cry out, *"Daddy, Father, You love me! You are Wealth — the God of more than enough. I am wealth — I have more than enough because I'm an heir of your glory!"*

When fear tries to grip your heart, cry out, *"Daddy, Father, You love me! You are my peace because I am an heir of your glory!"*

You and I are heirs of God's glory! If we truly believe that, we will experience overflowing joy, peace that passes understanding and security in a world that is very insecure. When we know who our Daddy is, no matter what comes against us, we will live safe and secure in His love. We will live confident that Who He is will manifest in our lives.

> Let's read Romans 8:31-32 again: *31 "What shall we say about such wonderful things as these? If God is for us, who can ever be against us? NLT*
>
> *32 He who did not withhold or spare [even] His own Son but gave Him up for us all, will He not also with Him freely and graciously give us all [other] things? AMP*

Verse 31: Have you ever heard such wonderful news as this: You were chosen, you were called, you were declared righteous by the King of kings and you are an heir of His glory! If your Daddy is for you – and He proved that He is – then who can be against you? No one! What foe can be against you or hold you back, if your Father God, the Great I Am, the Creator of the Universe, the King of kings, is for you? When you understand this truth, it won't matter what anyone else's opinion or judgment is toward you. Your Daddy is on your side! He believes in you! You have everything you need to reign in life through Jesus! Romans 8:32 assures you that if your Daddy loved you so much that He gave His Son for you, He will also freely and graciously give you all good things!

What did you learn today about being an heir of God's glory?

____

____

____

____

____

Why can you live safe and secure in His love?

____

____

____

____

Day 3

Nothing Can Separate You from His Love

Romans 8:33-39

Take time to pray before you begin.

Today we will finish our study of Romans chapter 8 as we continue to grow in our understanding of our Daddy's love for us.

> Romans 8:33-39: *33 Who shall bring any charge against God's elect [when it is] God Who justifies?...Who shall come forward and accuse or impeach those whom God has chosen? Will God, Who acquits us?] 34 Who is there to condemn [us]? Will Christ Jesus (the Messiah), Who died, or rather Who was raised from the dead, Who is at the right hand of God actually pleading as He intercedes for us? AMP 35 Can anything ever separate us from Christ's love? Does it mean he no longer loves us if we have trouble or calamity, or are persecuted, or hungry, or destitute, or in danger, or threatened with death? 36 (As the Scriptures say, "For your sake we are killed every day; we are being slaughtered like sheep.") 37 No, despite all these things, overwhelming victory is ours through Christ, who loved us. 38 And I am convinced (persuaded beyond doubt) that nothing can ever separate us from God's love. Neither death nor life, neither angels nor demons, neither our fears for today nor our worries about tomorrow – not even the powers of hell can separate us from God's love. 39 No power in the sky above or in the earth below – indeed, nothing in all creation will ever be able to separate us from the love of God that is revealed in Christ Jesus our Lord. NLT*

Can anyone bring a charge against you and accuse you? Why not? (verse 33)

____

____

Why is there no one who can condemn you? (verse 34)

____

____

Does it mean that God doesn't love you if you experience negative circumstances in your life? What is true of you according to verse 37?

____

____

What can you be absolutely sure of? (verse 38-39)

Your Daddy's opinion of you is all that matters!

Verse 33-34: If your Daddy, the King of kings has judged you free from all guilt and condemnation and declared you righteous is there anyone of higher authority that can bring a charge against you? No! He is the final authority and He has given you His judgment of innocence, forgiveness, and acquittal! Let no one judge you otherwise!

What your Daddy says about you is true! His good opinion of you is all that matters.

If your Father says you are beautiful, wonderful and perfect, then who can say otherwise? When the King of kings and Lord of lords has justified you and declared you righteous, who is mere man to have more authority over your life than the living God? If God isn't condemning you, then who can? By a judicial act of Almighty God, He has judged you in Christ as innocent, favored and blessed. When you fully embrace His good opinion of you, you'll find yourself free of the fear of what anybody else thinks.

One of the greatest fears that cause people to live insecure is the fear of what others think. I lived with that fear for years. I lived as a fearful slave, in bondage to other people's opinions. But when I began to embrace my true identity and agree with my Daddy's opinion of me, it didn't matter to me anymore what other people thought.

As a public speaker, I have had people say things about me that weren't very nice. Not too long ago I heard that someone had said, "I can't stand listening to her voice." In the past, I might have thought, "What's wrong with my voice? Should I talk differently?" But this time, I only thought about what they said for a brief moment, then I turned my thoughts to Jesus and said, "Father, You love my voice. You love to hear me speak. You even love to hear me sing." These thoughts put a smile on my face and filled my heart with peace. Suddenly, it didn't matter who came against me, or what their opinion of me was. What did matter was, "I know who my Daddy is, and He's the Judge of all judges. He has already judged me perfect and He thinks I have a beautiful voice. He says to me, 'How beautiful you are, My beloved. There is no flaw in you'" (Song of Songs 4:7). You and I don't have to live like a fearful slave wondering what everybody thinks of us. We can live confident that what our Daddy says about us is true and live secure in His love!

You are Victorious in Jesus!

> Let's read Romans 8:35 and 37 again, *"Can anything ever separate us from Christ's love? Does it mean he no longer loves us if we have trouble or calamity, or are persecuted, or hungry, or destitute, or in danger, or threatened with death? 37 No, despite all these things, overwhelming victory is ours through Christ, who loved us."*

Many times when we face negative circumstances in our lives it can cause us to question our Father's love for us. The enemy uses these situations to cause us to wonder if we can really trust that what our Father says is true.

Have you ever experienced a negative situation that caused you to question your Father God's love for you?

The truth is that no matter what life throws at you, whether it's financial struggles, danger, sickness or if even death, Jesus made you an overcomer because He loves you! It's His love for you that will comfort you through any trying situation and give you the grace to trust Him as you watch Him manifest His glory in your life.

There are two ways we can respond to trials in our lives:

1. Doubt God's love and goodness toward us and be discouraged and fearful; or

2. Remember that Jesus made us more than conquerors in every situation. We are heirs of the manifestation of Who God is in us! Nothing can defeat us because we are victorious through Him who loves us!

Nothing Can Separate You from His Love

Now let's end our study by reading the last two verses in Romans chapter 8.

> Romans 8:38-39: *38 And I am convinced [persuaded beyond doubt] that nothing can ever separate us from God's love. Neither death nor life, neither angels nor demons, neither our fears for today nor our worries about tomorrow — not even the powers of hell can separate us from God's love. 39 No power in the sky above or in the earth below — indeed, nothing in all creation will ever be able to separate us from the love of God that is revealed in Christ Jesus our Lord. NLT [Author's Insert]*

There is nothing that can ever separate you from your Daddy's love. His good opinion of you will never change, and He will be there to help you no matter what trial life brings. No matter what you do, He will always love you. He sent Jesus to purchase your freedom so that you could become His beloved child and live safe and secure in His great love!

Let's finish by reading Romans 8:31-39 in the Message Bible:

> Romans 8:31-39: *31 So, what do you think? With God on our side like this, how can we lose? 32 If God didn't hesitate to put everything on the line for us, embracing our condition and exposing himself to the worst by sending his own Son, is there anything else he wouldn't gladly and freely do for us? 33 And who would dare tangle with God by messing with one of God's chosen? 34 Who would dare even to point a finger? The One who died for us—who was raised to life for us!—is in the presence of God at this very moment sticking up for us. 35 Do you think anyone is going to be able to drive a wedge between us and Christ's love for us? There is no way! Not trouble,*

not hard times, not hatred, not hunger, not homelessness, not bullying threats, not backstabbing, not even the worst sins listed in Scripture: 36 They kill us in cold blood because they hate you. We're sitting ducks; they pick us off one by one. 37 None of this fazes us because Jesus loves us. 38 I'm absolutely convinced that nothing—nothing living or dead, angelic or demonic, today or tomorrow, 39 high or low, thinkable or unthinkable—absolutely nothing can get between us and God's love because of the way that Jesus our Master has embraced us. MSG

So Awake to Righteousness!

You are a beloved child of God, so you can boldly say, "I am fully persuaded beyond doubt that nothing will ever change my Daddy's good opinion of me. Nothing can ever separate me from His love that is revealed in Jesus! I am no longer a fearful slave, but a beloved child of God and an heir of His glory! Everything He has belongs to me! I am who my Father says I am! I am loved, righteous, qualified, blessed, favored, and perfect in His sight because of Jesus!

Holy Bible Special Hebrew-Greek Key Study Edition copyright © 1984 by Spiros Zodhiates and AMG International, Inc.

Merriam Webster's College Dictionary, 10th Edition
copyright © 1994 by Merriam-Webster, Inc.

Strong's Exhaustive Concordance of the Bible

Thorndike Barnhart Intermediate Dictionary

Vine's Expository Dictionary of New Testament Words

We would love to hear how this Bible Study has impacted your life.

To contact the author, write:

Connie Witter
Because of Jesus Ministries
P.O. Box 3064
Broken Arrow, OK 74013-3064

Or email:

Connie@becauseofJesus.com

For additional copies of this book go to:

www.becauseofJesus.com
Or call 918-994-6500

Connie Witter is a speaker, author, and Bible Study teacher. Her best selling book, *P.S. God Loves You,* has sold over 150,000 copies. She is the founder of *Because of Jesus Ministries* which was established in 2006 and has been teaching Bible Studies for over 20 years. Her Bible Study, *Because of Jesus,* was published in 2002 and is the foundation of her life and ministry. Since 2005, she has held an annual *Because of Jesus Women's Conference* in Tulsa and the outlying areas.

Connie has traveled throughout the United States and Russia, sharing the life-changing message of *Because of Jesus.* She has been the guest speaker at churches, women's conferences and retreats, and has also spoken into the lives of teenage girls. She has also been a guest on several Christian TV programs. Her weekly TV program, *Because of Jesus,* can be seen worldwide through her ministry website, *www.becauseofJesus.com.* Each week she shares the Good News: That we are righteous, valuable, precious, blessed, favored and extravagantly loved by God, because of Jesus. Thousands of lives have been changed through her ministry.

If you are interested in having Connie come speak at your event you can contact her at connie@becauseofjesus.com.

Other Bible Studies by Connie Witter

Awake to Righteousness Volume 2
Because of Jesus Bible Study
Living Loved Living Free Bible Study

Books by Connie Witter

P.S. God Loves You
21 Days to Discover Who You Are in Jesus
Living Loved Living Free
The Inside Story Teen Devotional
The Inside Story for Girls Devotional

CD/DVD Series by Connie Witter

Because of Jesus
Living Loved, Living Free
Awake to Righteousness Volume 1 and 2
It is Finished — A Study on the Book of Hebrews
Forsaking Religion Embracing Relationship: A Study on the Book of Galatians
Christ in You — The Hope of Glory: A Study on the Book of Colossians
God's Abundant Provision of Grace: Experiencing Financial Freedom in Christ
Psalm 23

To order any of these products go to: www.becauseofjesus.com

Notes